Nancy from
Grandmother

Christmas, 1965.

It seems to give significance
to this book that someone
else owned and loved it before.
It was difficult to find
a copy but I couldn't
rest until I did because
I wanted it for you, my
dear Philena. Because you
have such courage and
strength you will
understand these verses.
The book comes to you
with my deepest love.
                    Mother

June 1968

POEMS *of*
Inspiration
AND Courage

POEMS *of* Inspiration AND Courage

The Best Verse of
GRACE NOLL CROWELL

Harper & Row, PUBLISHERS

NEW YORK

TO MY KIND FRIEND AND LONG-TIME EDITOR

Eugene Exman

ACKNOWLEDGMENTS

All of the material in this book has been published in the following volumes published by Harper & Row, Publishers, Incorporated.

Apples of Gold, 1950; *Between Eternities,* 1944; *Bright Harvest,* 1952; *The Crystal Fountain,* 1948; *Facing the Stars,* 1941; *Flame in the Wind,* 1930, 1934; *Journey into Dawn,* 1955; *The Lifted Lamp,* 1942; *Light of the Years,* 1936; *The Radiant Quest,* 1940; *Silver in the Sun,* 1928, 1934; *Some Brighter Dawn,* 1943; *Songs for Comfort,* 1937, 1939, 1941, 1943, 1946, 1947; *Songs for Courage,* 1938; *Songs of Faith,* 1939; *Songs of Hope,* 1938; *Songs of Triumph,* 1946, 1955, 1956, 1957, 1959; *Splendor Ahead,* 1940; *White Fire,* 1934; *The Wind-Swept Harp,* 1946; *This Golden Summit,* 1937.

FIRST EDITION

Library of Congress Catalog Card Number: 65-20448

Contents

v

vi

Introduction

As a labor of love, this collection of the works of the beloved American poet has been compiled. Selections have been chosen for their power to console in times of tribulation and to enlarge our capacity for joy in life and faith in God. There are poems of courage and inspiration, of the glory and wisdom of creation, and of the comfort we have in living in the world of the imagination.

Grace Noll Crowell has had a truly remarkable life—her books of prose and poetry mirror a lifetime of distilled wisdom, faith, and consolation. Her writings arouse admiration, and this deeply satisfying treasury of her works will be a comfort to readers of all faiths and creeds.

Mrs. Crowell has been writing verse since 1906, and her work has been published in *Good Housekeeping, The Christian Herald, The New York Times, The Christian Science Monitor, McCall's,* and many other magazines and journals, both in this country and in England. She has won many prizes in poetry contests. More than thirty-five published books have come from her pen.

—BLISS ALBRIGHT

Foreword

The poems in this volume were selected from my published work with my personal attention and approval. They have been chosen with my hope that the reader may find certain poems, written from my own experience of life, helpful and comforting.

The nature lyrics have been included to give a balance of subject matter, trusting that they may bring to the reader a feeling of refreshment and renewal.

At any rate, the book goes out with my blessing for any reader who may find inspiration and courage within its contents.

—GRACE NOLL CROWELL

Dallas, Texas

POEMS *of*
Inspiration
AND Courage

A SONG FOR ANY PILGRIMAGE

I shall start before the dawn
Any pilgrimage I make;
I shall watch the day move on;
I shall watch the world awake;

I shall travel with the sun,
Travel lightly, travel free,
I shall speak to every one
Who may turn and speak to me.

I shall drink the morning dew;
I shall break noon's golden bread,
And at night the dark will strew
Soft warm blankets for my bed.

I shall bathe beside a brook;
By my candle's light shall read
Words within a little book
That I carry for my need.

I shall snuff my candle out,
Pray the Lord my soul to keep,
Then without a fear or doubt
Make the pilgrimage of sleep.

God wrote His loveliest poem on the day
He made the first tall silver poplar tree,
And set it high upon a pale-gold hill
For all the new enchanted earth to see.

I think its beauty must have made Him glad,
And that He smiled at it—and loved it so—
Then turned in sudden sheer delight and made
A dozen silver poplars in a row.

Mist-green and white against a turquoise sky,
Ashimmer and ashine they stood at noon;
A misty silver loveliness at night.
Breathless beneath the first small wistful moon.

And then God took the music of the winds,
And set each leaf aflutter and athrill—
Today I read His poem word by word
Among the silver poplars on the hill.

"The day will bring some lovely thing,"
I say it over each new dawn:
"Some gay, adventurous thing to hold
Against my heart when it is gone,"
And so I rise and go to meet
The day with wings upon my feet.

I come upon it unaware:
Some sudden beauty without name:
A snatch of song, a breath of pine,
A poem lit with golden flame;
High tangled bird notes, keenly thinned,
Like flying color on the wind.

No day has ever failed me quite:
Before the grayest day is done
I find some misty purple bloom,
Or a late line of crimson sun.
Each night I pause—remembering—
Some gay, adventurous, lovely thing.

I saw a valiant cardinal
Dark-red against the winter dawn,
He whistled from a leafless tree
Upon a barren lawn.

The tiny dauntless splotch of red
Shot up a challenge straight and high:
A rocket-burst of silver stars
To shower a winter sky.

The little brave intrepid thing:
A conqueror of cold and night.
He drenched the bare boughs suddenly
With color and with light.

A triumph and a victory
That I have come to understand.
I laughed—a broken laugh—and took
Life once more by the hand.

The mockingbird is music-mad tonight,
He thinks the stars are notes;
That he must sing each spattered star, and be
A choir of many throats.

The earth is his cathedral, and its dome
Is all the light-pricked sky,
The pear tree is his choir loft, and there
He flings his mad song high.

The moon-white blossoms are young girls to him,
Who kneel at night to pray;
The buds, their rosaries, the little winds
Are whispered prayers they say.

He thinks he is the whole cathedral choir,
And bursts his little throat;
I lie awake—and do not breathe—lest I
May miss one single note.

FAITH

Faith is a brightness and a shining way—
Faith is a glory that the brave have worn,
Faith is a singing through the long gray day,
Faith is a healing for old hurts long borne;
Faith is the first white star hung low;
Faith is the ocean's moonlit sheen;
Faith is the dreams that all hearts know,
The evidence of things that are not seen.

I have not seen it—yet it walks with me;
I have not touched it—yet it holds my hand;
I shall not lose it through eternity
Whether my journey be by sea or land—
With its high torch to light the alien skies,
I shall face life and death with fearless eyes.

IMAGE

Standing upon the outposts of the world,
Shaping the stars and moon, molding the sun,
God, in the white heat of creation, hurled
The mountains into place, and called them done.
He set the seas in motion, found them good;
He watched the light and darkness as they ran
Smoothly beneath His fingers; then He stood
High on a pinnacle, and made a man.

In His own image made He him: a form
As beautiful as dawn when night is past;
He set the red blood coursing swift and warm,
Steadied the wild heartbeat, and then at last—
Intelligence! His far creation's goal,
With man's form housing an immortal soul.

BREAD

Some labor gathers to itself a light;
This I have found where women making bread
Perform anew an ancient, simple rite,
That men and little children might be fed.
Something about the handling of white flour
Is beautiful: the thought of sun on wheat;
The shining silver of a quick, late shower,
A great mill glimmering through the harvest heat.

And old as life, a fadeless picture still,
The gold of grain crushed fine beneath a stone;
Two women grinding at an ancient mill,
And one is taken, one is left alone,
O, always, somewhere, women have made bread,
That men and little children might be fed.

This morning as I climbed a golden hill
I came upon a slim crabapple tree:
A pink-white cloud of glory . . . I stood still—
For like a runner, breath was gone from me.
It was the loveliest, the gayest thing
That ever graced a sunny crest in spring!

I closed my eyes—there was no sound save one:
The warm gold hum of weighted honey bees;
There was only a crab tree blossoming in the sun,
And a faintly perfumed, petal-rippling breeze,
And laughter, running along the slopes of light
To catch me in a shower of pink and white.
Yet I stood breathless in the shimmering spray
As if I, too, had run a long, long way.

THREE SONNETS

1. BIRTH

The dark, a light, a quick and strangling cry;
A far faint voice, the touch of a deft, clean hand,
A smoothness blanketing this small thing called "I,"
Who am a pilgrim out of the shadowland.
A hunger-wail, and lips to a fragrant breast:
The milk and honey after a long dark night,
And sleep comes down—a pilgrim has need of rest
For eyes grown blind in the glare of a sudden light.

O, what is Life but the beat of a small red heart?
And what is Life but a quick and strangling cry?
And how does a warm, sweet-flowing breast have part
In the essence of this immortal thing called "I"?
I am a pilgrim, and a pilgrim goes
Asking the way of Life, and no one knows.

2. LIFE

And now that I have wandered many miles
Down many a road, and many a crooked lane,
And know Life is a thing of tears and smiles,
Of peace, and white-winged joy, and bitter pain,
Yet should some brother ask the way to go,
I could not tell him, nor which road is best,
I do not know his way, I only know
That every road and every trail leads West.

No one can go the way that I have gone,
I cannot go where other far trails run.
Through light and shadow Life has beckoned on
Into the glories of the setting sun.
The way I go, no other feet have trod,
And no one walks the road with me but God.

3. DEATH

Not knowing Life, how can I well know Death?
Yet when he comes, I think that I shall be
Tiptoe upon a shore, with bated breath,
Watching a broad gold path lead out to sea.
The sun will gild the spires of the town;
Clear bells will call the village folk to prayer;
The sudden summer darkness will drop down,
And I shall turn, and see Death standing there.

The shadows will be very deep that night,
But O, I trust I shall not be afraid.
Perhaps Death carries in his hand a light—
These are the things for which I long have prayed,
And looking in his face that I shall see
The one friend who has walked the road with me.

Since I have had a son
I cannot pray—
"God keep my son," unless I say:
"God keep all mothers' sons
This day."

Since I have had a son
I cannot see
Another's son hurt needlessly,
But the mother-heart is torn
In me.

All mothers' sons are mine
Since I have had
This gray-eyed, laughing little lad.
I love them all—the good,
The bad.

All mothers' sons are mine,
And so I say:
"God keep the sons of earth this day.
Shield them from needless hurt,
I pray."

14

Unseen by human eyes
Are the arsenals of strength:
Whether it be a tree's root,
Its strong and reaching length,
Or in a flower's growth
Springing up from the sod—
These are the arsenals
Equipped by the hand of God.

Unseen by earthly eyes
Are the forces in man's heart,
Where courage dwells, and faith's
Hidden bright springs start,
Where hope lies rooted deep
Waiting the seed's quick swell—
This is man's inner strength,
This is God's arsenal.

There is a green light over the land.
In the sharp wind the bare boughs shiver,
Huddled together the young colts stand,
And yet there is an exquisite quiver
Of pale-green light in the heady wind:
Caught in its brittleness, a flowing
Of apple-green that is sharply thinned
Where once but tawny weeds were growing.

Wheat! The wheat! Sown long to lie
Alone beneath the wind's white drifting.
Under the gusty wintry sky
Its sudden inch-high spears are lifting.
And soon beneath the rain and sun
The jointed stalks, the full grain bending:
A promise kept, and work well done,
And a field at rest at the summer's ending.

And here, this moment, the air is rife,
And the land is pregnant with age-old meaning:
Here is the substance, the form of life;
Here is the hope of a golden gleaning.

This is the path worn bare by many feet:
My father's feet who sought his fields at dawn:
My mother, who would stop to smell the sweet
Wild clover blooming here, and then move on,
Helped make this small meandering path that goes
Its crooked way across the hills and down,
Arched here and there by fennel and wild rose;
Yet still the earth beneath lies packed and brown.

How many childhood mornings I have run
Along this path, my feet scarce touching ground;
The sweet insistent wind, the caressing sun
Brushing my face, with only the lisping sound
Of grass and weeds as I went on swift wing
Helping create this lovely lasting thing.

A strange surprising gladness stirs my heart
At night when heaven's first lights, dim and far,
Swing in the dusk—and each one suddenly
Becomes the silver wonder of a star.

Becomes a shining splendor on the hills:
Unfailing, steadfast, calm and high and white,
Stars are so beautiful, so steeped in peace,
They rest me more than anything at night.

There is an ancient comfort in the stars:
I treasure it, "Lift up your eyes and see,"
"He calleth them by name, not one hath failed. . . ."
O, often through His stars God comforts me.

Friends are like flowers. I have found them so:
The hardy staunch perennials that grow
Year after year are like some friends I know.

One need not cultivate them with great care,
They only need the sun and wind and air
Of trust and love, and they are always there.

Some must be nursed with frequent trowel and spade,
And sheltered from the sun or too much shade,
For fear their frail and clinging bloom may fade,

Friends are like flowers. I would be a friend
Whose blossomings no hand need ever tend:
A perennial on whom hearts can depend.

We do not tell the things that hurt us most.
Our moving tongues release a motley host
Of small inconsequential words—We say:
"Oh, I am fine." "It is a lovely day . . ."
The hidden grief we bear we never tell
We go our several ways, dissembling well.

Only to One who listens as we speak,
From One alone, who has the power, we seek
For comfort and for peace, and find it there.
We touch His robe, His hand rests on our hair,
And often the grief is lessened, often gone,
But always the strength is given to go on.

SOME BETTER THING

O Heart, if seemingly God has not answered
Some anguished cry, some earnest seeking prayer,
Do not rebel and say, "He is not mindful."
And, O dear heart, try never to despair.
Although the words themselves be left unuttered,
Through agony too great for tongue to say,
Even the unvoiced prayer He hears and answers,
If not in your way—in some better way.

"Some better thing," He promises to give you:
Better than you could ask or think. Be still
And wait and hope and trust, for in that giving
Will be the answer to His blessed will.
Far more than any prayer that you could bring
He will encompass in that "better thing."

A child looked up with his earnest eyes:
"Where does the light of a candle go
When I blow it out?" and not being wise
I only could answer: "I do not know."

"It was so little and bright," he said,
"And now it's so little and lost . . ." and I,
Turning to tuck him into bed,
As puzzled as he, could not reply.

"So little and bright—so little and lost—"
Over and over the brief words came,
A moment ago a candle tossed
Here in this room a vital flame—

Where is it now, and where are we
When our lives are blown out by the casement wind?
Nothing is lost—it cannot be,
Our souls must be flames, released and thinned,

Making their sure way through the dark,
Climbing the chasms, cleaving the night,
To be cupped by the hand of God somewhere,
And steadied by Him for eternal light.

JESUS WAS A POET

J esus was a poet—
He spoke in singing words
Of gold wheat and its sowing,
Of little feathered birds;
He told of one repentant
Who had set himself to roam,
And many a pilgrim, harking,
Has wept and turned toward home.

He sang of vine and fig tree,
Of water and of bread,
Of sheep and a good shepherd,
And every word He said
Is pregnant with deep meaning
To pierce the listener through:
Strong words that live forever
As great poetry should do.
And though no single stanza
Has balanced form or rhyme,
Yet Jesus is the greatest
Poet of all time.

THINKING

"Whatsoever things are lovely"—
We are told to think on these.
I shall think of quiet waters,
Of clean winds and blossoming trees,
Of the countless things of beauty
I have watched upon my knees.

"Whatsoever things are true"—Lord,
I shall find them in Thy word,
I shall con their meaning over
With my spirit deeply stirred
As I think of all the blessings
In the good news I have heard.

And the things, Lord, that are honest,
Just and pure down troubled ways . . .
I shall think of men and women
Walking upright through their days;
I shall think of Thee, Lord, working
For our good, and give Thee praise.

"HE THAT KEEPETH THEE"

So often in the dark hours of the night
It comforts me to know of One who stays
Close by my side, whose presence is a light
And a strength and solace through my nights and days.
And I am blest to know that as I sleep
He watches tenderly above me there,
And if I lie awake He stays to keep
Me comraded and safe within His care.

O Love that will not slumber when my need
Is great through wearing pain or bitter loss,
O Love compassionate enough to heed
My cry, and with the strength to lift the cross
That otherwise might crush me—Love divine,
I thank Thee for this constant care of Thine.

PILGRIM

I shall plant the seed of this fruit on which I dine
By the side of the road—perhaps someday a tree
Will lift its leafy boughs, and its fruit will shine
Down a bleak autumn evening goldenly.

I shall place these sticks together, and some gray day
One following me may see them and pause to start
A quick bright fire along his lonely way,
And its wind-blown flame may warm his hands and his heart.

I shall pencil a pointing finger where a spring
Leaps silverly among the rock-strewn grass;
Others will need its clear cold offering,
And perhaps they might fail to see it as they pass.

At the bend of the road I shall build a wayside shrine,
Stone by stone I shall rear it and leave it there,
It may be that some one whose need is as great as mine
May seek it and find new comfort and strength in prayer.

Sun-up and sun-down,
And between them the high blue arc of the sky,
And the hours that are to be lived, and I
The one who must live them . . . Oh, my heart,
Let us do splendidly our part;
God has done His: His clean hand turns
A golden dial, and the dawn sun burns;
And the day is here with its glad surprise,
Unsullied and clean. Oh, heart be wise!
Oh, heart be strong as you take your way
Into this glorious unlived day;
Keep it beautiful, keep it fine,
Splendidly lived hours shine and shine
Like silver disks in a slanting sun
Long after the day is past and done.
Hold them, heart, for remembering . . .
A clean new day is a wonderful thing!

AT THE GATE

There is a lovely picture that I see,
As clear and clean-cut as a cameo:
My mother, waiting at the gate for me
Long ago:

A picket gate where yellow roses grew,
The scent of plum blooms fragrant on the air;
Bright leaves above her, the sun shining through,
Lighting her hair.

And I am coming down the old home street:
A shaded street where arching maples were,
A little girl on lightly running feet,
Coming to her.

Oh, often now, when weary of the road
That leads me home, I pause and breathe a prayer
That by some gateway at the close of day
She will be there.

Shading her eyes against the heavenly light,
Peering along a heavenly street to see
That she may catch the first, fluttering white
Glimpse of me.

DEFINITION

I search among the plain and lovely words
To find what the one word "Mother" means;
    as well
Try to define the tangled song of birds;
The echo in the hills of one clear bell.
One cannot snare the wind, or catch the wings
Of shadows flying low across the wheat;
Ah, who can prison simple, natural things
That make the long days beautiful and sweet?

"Mother"—a word that holds the tender spell
Of all the dear essential things of earth;
A home, clean sunlit rooms, the good smell
Of bread; a table spread; a glowing hearth.
And love beyond the dream of anyone . . .
I search for words for her . . . and there are none.

Here is such rapture,
Here is such delight;
Water birds preening
For a morning flight.
Exquisitely chiseled
Upon the shore sands,
Water for its mirror,
One heron stands.
Startling its beauty,
Startling its pose,
Reeds whistle sharply—
A wild goose goes,
Gray wings flapping,
Gray wings spread,
Bright on the water
The dawn burns red.
Up from the rushes
Strong wings whir,
A silence is settling
Where they were,
Long lines leaving
The dawn-lit sands,
Still beside its mirror
One heron stands.

If you have never seen cranes flying
You cannot dream
How the high wind tangles with their crying,
How they gleam.

Oh, you have missed so much—beyond believing!
Cranes are so white,
They have such a magical way of weaving
Lines of light;

They have such an exquisite way of finding
Paths through skies,
A white and black dazzling way of blinding
Watching eyes;

Such a quivering, quivering way of making
Gray days bright—
Cranes in a high line have a way of taking
Breath and sight.

THE OLD FAMILIAR THINGS

With all the world in turmoil and the days
Strange cluttered lengths of clamor and of strife,
I like to think old fundamental ways
Still hold their rhythm in the scheme of life;
That with a sweet insistence through the years
Unfailingly love lifts its dauntless song;
That laughter sounds a stronger note than tears;
And right is clearer-throated, far, than wrong.

The music of the wind and of the rain
Still runs lighthearted down the ancient fields;
There is a flowing melody in grain,
And praises rise above the loaves it yields.
Forever there is poetry that sings
Through all earth's old familiar lovely things.

Symbols of faith, they lift their reaching spires
Above green groves down many a country way,
And on the wide plains there are altar fires
That light the forms of those who kneel to pray.
And I have seen them stand knee-deep in wheat:
White country churches, rising from the sod,
Where men, in gratitude for bread to eat,
Have paused, and reared their altars to their God.

Symbols they are to mankind's daily need:
The urgent need to pray, the need to praise.
Without their altars, men grow blind indeed,
And grope, bewildered, down unlighted ways.
The look of God is over every land
Where men have toiled, and where their churches stand.

Pedro is brown from the suns of Old Mexico.
His face is pitted from past disease.
He stands in the aisle of a busy store
Before a table heaped with cheap prints.

The pictures have gaudily gilded frames
About fruit more red and yellow
Than ever ripens in earthly orchards.
There are ugly-shaped pitchers
Filled with stiff, unnamable flowers,
And landscapes greener than the greenest spring;

But Pedro does not see them.
His dark smoldering eyes
Have come to rest upon the pictured face
Of the Christ,
His own Christ, hanging tortuously
Upon a jagged cross,
With patient eyes uplifted
In mute agony—for the sins of Pedro.

Involuntarily
The hard rough hands move
To form a cross.

The price is plainly marked above the prints;
So pitifully little, so pitifully much.
There is only a small crumpled bill

In Pedro's soiled pocket:
One dollar,
And it should buy bread and fruit
For Maria and for little Antonio:
Maria, who is often ailing,
And Antonio, who hurts Pedro daily
Because he does not run and play
As do the other boys of the street.

Bread and fruit—
Bread—and fruit—
Or—the compassionate, white Christ
To take to the little room
To hang there above a glimmering, lighted candle.

Suddenly—
Into Pedro's troubled eyes there has come quietness.
The crumpled bill passes from his hands.
He grasps his package with reverent fingers,
And is lost from me in the throng,
And someway—
I, who am of another nation, and another creed,
Am close akin to Pedro.
My need is also greater
For the continuous presence
Of the White Christ in my little room,
Than for bread or for fruit—this day.

Has anyone seen him? Where did he go?
I lost him, oh, ever so long ago.
Tell them to search for him, I cannot say
What road he took when he went away.
Tell them to watch down each alley and street:
Ways he went often on light, flying feet;
Look through the meadows where he used to run,
Follow where silver streams leap in the sun;
Search for him everywhere, he is so small,
One might pass by and not see him at all;
But if they find a boy—if his eyes shine,
If his hair blows in the wind, he is mine.
If he is laughing, dancing with joy,
They may be sure that he is my boy.
Tell them to search down the world's farthest track,
And oh, if they find him—please bring him back.

I shall store within my soul today
Some precious sunny bit of cheer
In case tomorrow's clouds be gray,
Its wind blow cold, its leaves be sere,
And my soul be a barren place
With a desolate world before my face.

Some sweet reserve of cheerfulness
To draw upon if grief be sore,
Or if, perchance, an old distress
Comes seeking welcome at my door.
The sun-room of my soul shall hold
Rich treasures from today's bright gold.

Thus hour by hour, God help me bring
Some golden gleaning till at last
My grief be but a song to sing,
My old distress as something past,
And better still, enough, I pray,
To share with those who pass my way.

A SONG FOR COMFORT

The things that are too hard to bear
God does not bid me bear.
I never yet have walked alone
Through dark hours of despair,
And always He has kept His word:
The promised strength was there.

And so today, my heart, be still,
He knows that you are torn,
He also knows that even this
Great sorrow can be borne.
His voice still speaks across the years:
"Blessed are they that mourn."

The grief that is too hard to bear
We need not bear, or fear,
Be comforted, remembering
That One who cares is near,
And He will hold us by the hand
Until the dark skies clear.

EVENING

When I go home across the hills at evening,
My little flock of dreams all gathered in—
A gentle peace and quietness will settle
Along the pathways where I late have been.
I will look backward and be glad, remembering
My perfect day, my lovely, wondrous day,
Forgetting then the high noon's fretful glaring,
The weariness of soul, the dusty way.
I will forget the climb to distant hilltops;
I will forget the chasms I have crossed,
And, O, I trust that I will have forgotten
Each little dream-white lamb that I have lost.

When I go home across the hills at evening,
One far, clear twilight bell will call to prayer,
And I will pause on some green close-cropped hillside,
And with high-lifted face will worship there.
I will tell Him, the great, good listening Shepherd,
How I have loved my beautiful, bright day:
The shell-pink sweetness of the dawning morning,
The flower faces that have starred my way;
The truant playing winds across the valleys;
The tender green within the crannied wall;
The stillness of the far cloud ship a-sailing—
The poignant beauty of a wild bird's call;

And suddenly—the first faint star will tremble,
A crescent moon will smile down tenderly—
And there, at last—through the soft purple twilight—
The near, dear lights of home will shine for me.

A STAR

A star has stopped above my heart—
I am aware
Of silver dust upon my face,
And in my hair;
I feel the star-points lengthening
Along the air.

A star has stopped above my heart—
So blinding, white,
I cannot see, I cannot breathe
It is so bright;
It blooms, this silver annual
Each Christmas night.

A star has stopped above my heart:
A flower in flame,
The same star that stood over Him
The night He came.
I turn, the quick tears in my eyes
And call His name.

How young He was, how short His time on earth!
A pulse-beat through the centuries, a breath
Between the starlit hour of His birth
And that strange darkened hour of His death.

Yet had those years not gone their swift sure way,
Had their significance been lost to men,
There would be darkness in the land today,
No faith would lift, no heart could hope again.

Thank God, thank God for those years' precious store!
Thank God for sparing Him to you, to me,
"Out of the glory that was theirs before
The world was . . ." and the glory yet to be.

The darkened years for Him, that brought us light;
The weary years for Him, that gave us rest;
The clamorous years, that we might know the white
High silences of peace within the breast.

For thirty-three brief years that His feet trod
The earthly roads for us, we thank Thee, God.

THERE IS A ROOM

My problem is so great today,
There is a room where I must go
And close the door, and kneel and pray,
And only God will know.

A room where often I have knelt
And agonized, and prayed, and plead,
Until, all comforted, I felt
God's hand upon my head.

A room I seek when I am glad
To thank the giver of it all.
Without Him I would not have had
These joys I have at all.

Within my house is one small room,
A haven from distress and care,
I turn to it, and through the gloom
Seek God—and find Him there.

Slowly I have learned that God answers prayer.
Slowly I have learned this vital thing:
That my petition loosed upon the air
Will reach its destination and will bring
The answer that will be the best for me inevitably.

Slowly, oh, so slowly I have learned
To wait the answer coming soon or late;
So often in the past I prayed, then turned,
Refusing in my eagerness to wait,
Yet even so the good God, who had heard,
Answered every word.

Surely I should wait patiently today,
Knowing the answered prayer is on its way.

DUCKS ON A POND

I saw a pond in the meadow grass
As motionless as a sheet of glass,
And on its breast three ducks afloat:
Each duck an iridescent boat
Of blue and green, of dun and brown;
And in the water, upside down,
Were three more duck as still and clear
As were the right-side-up ones . . .   Queer.
How beautiful it was to me,
That windless, bright tranquility!

A wild exhilaration in their wings,
The martins fly;
Like swift dark arrows shot from unseen bows,
They pierce the sky;
They swoop and drop and circle as they climb
Into the light
That is half crimson day, and half blue dusk
Of the coming night.

The air is filled with the flicker of beating wings—
There is no cry,
Only the silent ecstasy of birds
As they wheel and fly;
Only an unshouted rapture, yet the hour
Is strangely loud
With motion—until the last wing is lost
Within a cloud.

He ever moved with heart and mind aflame,
Searching the woodlands for some faerie thing,
Striving to capture that without a name:
Light on a bird's throat, color upon a wing.
The metallic glitter of a wood duck's crest,
The snow-white floating stillness of a swan,
The burning orange in an oriole's nest
Drew out the very heart of Audubon.

A golden eagle on an autumn day
Spiraling downward in the yellow light,
A scarlet grosbeak in an emerald spray
Of misty leaves—these were his fierce delight.
To paint them all—his passionate desire,
And with his brush he wrote his name in fire.

The poplar tree at the garden gate
Reaches through moonlight, straight and tall,
A great star quivering at its tip
Like molten fire ready to fall.

The wind is silver that stirs the leaves,
And silver the tinkling tune it makes,
While out of a mockingbird's small throat
Silvery-clear a high bell shakes.

One slender tree by a garden gate,
A luminous wind, and a bird's tossed bell,
And I, who had thought I would never again
Be moved by beauty, staggered and fell,

Pierced to the heart with an old delight
Sharp as a sword, and glad to be
Wounded that I might rise again
Out of a long strange apathy.

I pray each morning that I be not blind
To the Christ who moves that day among my kind.
I dare not turn a hungry man away,
Lest I be leaving Him unfed today.
I dare not slight some tattered, unclothed one
Lest I should fail to warm and clothe God's Son.
I cannot pass one languishing in bed,
Lest it be Jesus lying there instead.

And every burden-bearer that I see
Must have my help, for oh, it might be He.
I must walk softly on the road today
I could meet Christ down any traveled way.

THE POET

Out of the highest agonies of pain;
Out of the holiest sorrows he must come;
From passion unto passion he must gain
The heights beyond the heights—and standing dumb
Within the awful silence of the past,
Burst into song—so winged with flame—so free—
That every tired heart will say: "At last—
Some one has found my voice—and sings for me."

TO A YOUNG POET

This one would say to you who long has known
The long hard road that lies before you there:
To be a poet you must walk alone
The darkened highways of the world—must share
The crust of beggars, and the crown of kings,
Earth's wild high laughter, and its bitter tears,
If you would have a lyric throat that sings;
If you would have your voice sound down the years.

Oh, Youth, if willingly you face this way,
Prepare your heart for hurt, your back for thongs,
For beauty will smite you fiercely day by day
And life's wine-press will crush you for your songs.
If you can face it—then, when all is said,
Go forward with God's blessing on your head.

A CANDLE

A candle is a lovely thing
To light for Him tonight:
A slim, white candle, straight and tall,
To make the darkness bright.

So white He was, so tall and straight,
That all the dark was lit:
A pathway widening on ahead
When He walked into it.

A candle burning in the night!
A symbol of the One
Who shed a glow of circling light
Until His work was done—

Then flickering out upon a cross,
Upon a darkened hill,
It lit again, the Light of Earth,
And it is burning still.

BECAUSE OF THY GREAT BOUNTY

Because I have been given much,
I, too, must give:
Because of Thy great bounty, Lord,
Each day I live
I shall divide my gifts from Thee
With every brother that I see
Who has the need of help from me.

Because I have been sheltered, fed,
By Thy good care,
I cannot see another's lack
And I not share
My glowing fire, my loaf of bread,
My roof's safe shelter overhead,
That he, too, may be comforted.

Because love has been lavished so
Upon me, Lord,
A wealth I know that was not meant
For me to hoard,
I shall give love to those in need,
Shall show that love by word and deed,
Thus shall my thanks be thanks indeed.

God let me find the lonely ones
Among the throng today,
And let me say the word to take
The loneliness away.
So many walk with aching hearts
Along the old highway.

So many walk with breaking hearts,
And no one understands;
They find the roadway rough and steep
Across the barren lands.
God help me lighten weary eyes
And strengthen nerveless hands.

God help me brighten dreary eyes,
And let my own grief be
A sure reminder of the grief
Of those who walk with me.
When words fail, hands fail, let me go
In silent sympathy.

YOUNG NUN

She is so young for this grave sacrifice!
I wonder by what winding roads she came
To these dark corridors? Some pay the price,
And 'tis not strange; but what white blowing flame
Drove her before it? What importunate voice
Pierced youth's wild delirium and drew
Her forward to this passionate high choice
Of service to a church a lifetime through?

The soft curves of her body hide beneath
The folds of her dark habit; yet her slim
Bright youthfulness is like a silver sheath.
Was there some lover? Does she think of him?
Or is that luminous fire in her eyes,
That still white light upon her lifted face,
A love, beyond earth's passion and surprise,
Set like a candle flame to light this place?

THE BRIDE

As slim and straight as the candles at her side
She stands, a flower with a flower's own grace.
Sheathed in the petaled satin of a bride,
Wrapped in a shimmering mist of fragile lace,
Serious and shy and very sweet,
She waits her lover's coming, eyes abrim
With happy dreams that are not yet complete
And only can be realized through him.

Here on the threshold of the years she stands,
So soon to leave her girlhood in the past.
God give her lover tender heart and hands
That the white radiance in her eyes may last;
God give her wisdom that she, too, may hold
His love till all the fires of earth grow cold.

THE LIFTED LAMP

I shall light my lamp at faith's white spark
And through this wild storm hold it high;
Perhaps across the utter dark
Its light will glow against the sky,
Steady enough and clear enough
For some lost one to steer him by.

LOVE

Love has been dragged too often through the mire.
I would brush it clean and free it from the bars
That would detain it. I would set it up
High on a cool green hill beneath the stars,
Where the wind can blow the clinging dust away,
And the cool night wash it with its crystal dew.
It matters not what others make of love.
Mine shall be pure and beautiful for you.

My love is like the shimmer of the stars.
It has absorbed the radiance of the moon;
It has taken on the glory of the sun
That climbs the far blue glittering heights at noon.
I am jealous of the name of love. I long
To lift it high, to hold it like a flame,
That no unworthy thing may venture near
To tarnish the white splendor of its name.

THE EVENING MEAL

The preparation of an evening meal
By any woman, anywhere, may be
A ceremony beautiful to see.

Recalling clear sweet evenings long ago
At Emmaus, or Bethany when One
Beloved guest had come at set of sun.

And oh, that other April evening meal,
Within an Upper Room—the grace He said
Above the scarlet wine, the broken bread!

An evening meal should be a gracious thing,
It matters not how plain may be the fare,
So long as love and loyalty are there.

The supper hour: a magnet drawing home
The ones who have the need of food and rest.
All women know this hour of day is best.

JAN VERMEER

(Dutch painter, 1632–75)

A lover of light, he ever sought to hold
The sunshine quivering on a window ledge,
Or to catch the evanescent glint of gold
That filtered in a room through tree and hedge,
And trembled like blown water there. The glaze
Of a crusted loaf, a bowl of milk abrim,
A cup's highlight, a pitcher's spangled rays—
These simple home-sweet subjects challenged him.

He painted women ever at some task,
The sun's own glory in their eyes and hair,
Serene and tranquil; nothing they could ask
Would make them more content . . . and so aware
Was the artist, that his canvases are rife
With the everlasting substances of life.

CATHEDRAL BELLS

(St. Louis Cathedral, New Orleans)

The sweet bright music trembles above the city
Where slow-struck metal sends its quivering voice
Above mankind, in need of love and pity,
Bidding hearts make a high and holy choice.
As clear as crystal in their silver singing
The bells continue their unhurried call
Across the Vieux Carré, their echoes ringing
From court and patio and moss-grown wall.

The hard beset humanity that surges
Down shuttered lane and narrow teeming street
Gives heed unconsciously to sound that purges
The mote-filled air; that sends out high and sweet
The clear assurance from its silver store
That it has voiced a century or more.

AVE MARIA

The organ's gold throat breathes a sacred name
As soft as the whispering wind across the wheat
That runs subdued through shadows, yet aflame
With ecstasy, devout and heavenly sweet.
Guilmont's Ave Maria—clear as bells
The pipes give back an echoing high cry
That rises and falls as the music dips and swells,
Then softens to a low-voiced lullaby.

"Beloved art thou . . ." The vaulted ceiling drips
With mellow music, and the frescoed walls
Make answer from a score of golden lips;
The ancient joyous salutation falls
Reiterating word by glorious word:
"Ave Maria . . . Mother of our Lord."

DENOMINATIONS

We come to God by devious ways,
And who am I to say
That the road I take is the only road,
My way, the better way.

The earnest seeker after God
Can find Him like a flame,
Down any road, no matter what
His creed, or what his name,

So whether we may pause to pray
Where great cathedrals shine,
Or in some little weathered church,
Or at a wayside shrine,

The sincere traveler will arrive
Where the welcoming home lights shine,
Although the countless thousands take
A different road from mine.

THE POET'S INKPOT

Out of its Stygian depths he draws to light
A miracle of color. Strange! I peer
Within to mark what wizardry is here,
And lo, but a knobbed bottle, black as night.
Your dripping pen drips words as lustrous bright
As lacquered gold upon tall moonlit spires,
And burning words that glow like liquid fires,
And words as cold as stars, aloof and white.

Poet, your inkpot yields such shining things,
And I love beauty so, and am so blind.
What fountain lies beyond this midnight brink
That mere words flash and gleam like lifted wings?
School me, O Poet, that I, too, may find
The source of beauty in my pot of ink.

The heart asks often: "What is poetry?
What is its essence? Where can it be found?"
And strange how vague the answer when we see
It in the new wheat lifting from the ground,
In a loaf of bread, in water from a spring,
Or in a plowshare deep in fertile loam,
In any simple fundamental thing
In constant daily use about a home.

We feel it in the wind among the corn,
We hear it in the dripping of the rain.
If loss of sight or sound makes one forlorn
The scent of apples, ripening down a lane,
Or a leaf fire smoke would be enough to tell
To any seeking one, that he may find
The meaning of the word through sense of smell,
Though he be stricken deaf and dumb and blind.

"Poetry must be as new as foam,
And as old as the rock," a philosopher once said.
His words still ring across the centuries
To listening poets though he long be dead.
"As new as foam," O words of mine, break white
And fresh and clean upon the shores of time;
May they be drawn from the unmeasured, deep
Ocean of life with its rhythm and its rhyme.

And may they be as old as the rocky cliffs
On which they leap and burst with ecstasy,
And may they hold the granite strength of truth
In their upward climb above life's lashing sea.
"As new as foam," as new and fresh as dawn,
Yet "old as the rock," O pen of mine, flow on!

UPON REARRANGING A SHELF OF OLD BOOKS

Almost I feel the pulse-beat of the ages,
Now swift, now slow, beneath my fingertips.
The heart-throbs of the prophets and the sages
Beat through these bindings, as my quick hand slips
Old books from dusty shelves in eager seeking
For truths that flaming tongues of the ancients tell;
For the words of wisdom that they still are speaking
As clearly as an echoing vesper bell.

Here is the melody that lies forever
At the deep heart of living; here we keep
The accurate, recorded discs that never
Can be quite silenced, though their makers sleep
The deep long sleep, so long as a seeker finds
The indelible imprint of their moving minds.

Oh, to live beautifully
For my brief hour
As does a wayside flower,
Unperturbed by the strange brevity
Of time allotted me;
Undisturbed by the overshadowing shine
Of tree and climbing vine;
Bravely stemming the wind and the beating rain,
Bowing and lifting again;
Within me some strong inner force as bright
As a poppy filled with light;
My feet firm-rooted in the earth's good sod,
My face turned toward God,
Yielding some fragrance down the paths I know
A little while . . . then go
As a flower goes, its petals seeking the ground
Without a cry or sound,
But leaving behind some gold seed lightly thinned
To blow upon the wind.

I questioned one who stood at the world's far crossroads:
"Which is the way that leads to Eternal Light?"
And he lifted his eyes to the hills ahead and answered:
"Yonder it lies, and the Guide is still in sight."
"Who is this Guide?" I asked, and he answered,
"Jesus."
"Who is this Jesus of whom I have never heard?"
And there to a lost, distressed and bewildered comrade
He told of the Saviour, word by precious word.

I left behind me the dark and troubled valley.
I took the road ahead and I found Him there:
A lamp to my feet, a radiance to my pathway;
And ever within my heart I am aware
That I might have missed the way at the far-off crossroads,
If one had failed me who had the words to say;
And I shall cry aloud to each hesitant pilgrim:
"Follow your Leader! Follow the Glory Way!"

ROADMATES

You who are my roadmates, you who go
Along the way with me, I do not know,
Save as I know myself. You have the same
Deep feeling that is mine—the inner flame
Of love for beauty, and a great capacity
For pity and compassion when you see
Another's hurt. You surely have, as I,
Known grief and sorrow as the years pass by,
And happiness and joy that lift the heart.
You must, as I have, often gone apart
To be alone with pain that none could share.
You question me: "How can you know?" you say,
And I make answer: "It is clear as day.
We are alike, made in God's image, so
Though you be stranger to me, yet I know."

AFTERNOON IN AN ART MUSEUM

(At a showing of Old Masters)

The late light sifts through corridors and halls.
The illumination from the ceiling globes
Sheds a subdued radiance on the walls,
And glows like fire upon the robes
Of saint and sinner. A deep midnight blue
Takes on the look of winter nights at sea,
The clear dark reds as if a flame shot through
A ruby's faceted intensity.

Old as the centuries each canvas speaks
A different language to the one who comes:
A young zealot, with eyes like live coals, seeks
For beauty in a strange delirium;
A scholar yonder cons a catalogue,
His monocle atilt, and strives to find
Within a painting, dimmed as if by fog,
Some new enlightenment to store in mind.
A surrealist with hands upon his hips
Pauses a moment, views this ancient art,
Then passes with a quip upon his lips
A work that once broke Botticelli's heart.
A young girl views the morning mist Corot
Had captured and had held throughout the years,
And something in that May day long ago
Akin to her has dimmed her eyes with tears.
I stand before a Rembrandt, view the Christ
Raised on a cross, stretched taut for all to see:

71

A square of paint, its glorious worth unpriced,
That draws the breath, the lifeblood out of me.
The shadows of the late December day
Deepen across the dome, the thundering street
Even in here has pressed its clamoring way—
I turn to seek it with reluctant feet,
Longing for men of my own time to find
The passion, inspiration, and the power
To paint, with color that will strike men blind,
Great truths to live beyond their own brief hour.

THERE IS A JOURNEY

There is a journey I must make:
From dawn to noon, from noon to dark
I must ascend and then descend
The shining pathway of an arc:
Up, up the golden hill to noon,
Then slowly down the slope toward night,
Not looking out beyond today
For guidance and for strength and light.

One little shining arc to tread—
Surely the way will not seem long
If I but pray for strength to go,
If I but lift a dauntless song,
If fortified by God's good grace
I tread the slope and make the climb
Light of heart and unafraid,
Living a moment at a time.

I shall keep some cool green memory in my heart
To draw upon should days be bleak and cold.
I shall hold it like a cherished thing apart
To turn to now or when I shall be old:
Perhaps a sweeping meadow, brightly green,
Where grasses bend and the winds of heaven blow
Straight from the hand of God, as cool and clean
As anything the heart of man can know.

Or it may be this green remembered tree
That I shall turn to if the nights be long,
High on a hill, its cool boughs lifting free,
And from its tip, a wild bird's joyous song.
A weary city dweller to survive
Must keep some cool green memory alive.

The brightness of the sunlight in your hair
Is like a lamp now suddenly blown out;
Your laughter through the rooms and on the stair,
Your high exuberance, your boyish shout
Are silenced, and old distant ivied walls
Have closed you in, and books with their demands
Lay hold upon you, and the future calls
To draw you forward with persistent hands.

Though the fabric of my mother love is strong,
I would not hold you by a single thread.
Go forward, keep your courage, keep your song
Of living clear, your bloodstream clean and red,
Your faith as high as always it has been,
Your values true—but O dear God, someway,
There is a victory, I too, must win
Over this strange fierce loneliness today!

She who lived valiantly has passed,
Why should we grieve,
Why should it break our hearts like this
If we believe?

Surely she lives more valiantly
Than ever before,
Freed, as she is, to move without
The weights she bore;

Freed for the sweet adventurings
Of heavenly days,
Lightened, to go exploring down
The glory-ways.

What must these first hours be to her
Who loved earth so?
How swift, how very swift and glad
Her feet must go!

She who lived valiantly has passed,
Why should we grieve?
Why should it break our hearts like this
If we believe?

I know that God hears prayer.
Although the burdens may
Seem greater than the heart can bear,
Still, day by day,
He eases them: a little here, a little there,
In answer, and some fitting hour
Along the road,
He stoops and lifts the load,
And bids us go, lighthearted, glad,
Stronger through testings we have had.

I know that God hears prayer.
We lift our praise,
And through his bright eternal days
The sound comes clear—
Like music to his ear.
Yea, every word of every prayer
Loosed on the air
Will bring an answer if we wait,
Though it come soon or late.

TO A JOURNEYING COMRADE

To you who are bearing a load up some steep hillside,
Burdened with grief and sorrow, or pain and care,
I have a word to say to you, O journeying comrade:
Do not despair.

You never can tell at all at what near turning
Some pleasant vista may meet your tired eyes
To lift your spirit up and dispel your weeping
With glad surprise.

You never can know what lies beyond a hilltop,
Perhaps some shadowy valley, cool and sweet,
Whose gentle downward sloping, after your climbing,
May rest your feet.

Always, O comrade, there is the chance that your burden
May slip from your back before the wayside dawn,
And O, my comrade, no matter how hard the going,
Keep on. Keep on!

Have you noticed, have you seen
That God loves green?
And that he loves clear yellow, too,
And blue—blue!
The trees, the sky, the glint of the sun,
The million yellow flowers that run
Their windy way;
And God loves gray:
The mist, the rain, the clouds that fly
When storms go by.
And looking at the dawn, I think
That God loves pink.
But red—have you ever thought how He
Uses it so sparingly?
A red flower here, another there,
A red wing flashing on the air,
A cluster of berries on a limb—
Red must be jewel-like to Him,
And very precious—but if I
Were asked the color I like best
'Twould be the color of the sky
Some autumn evening in the west:
Not mauve, not pink, not gold, not flame—
It has no name!

This intricate machine within the breast,
Set there to run untouched from birth to death—
I marvel at a thing that knows no rest
By day or night as long as there is breath.
God made a million things: the moon, the sun,
He flung the planets and the stars apart,
Created seas and mountains, and this done
Set at His master-task: the human heart.

A living, pulsing, wild tempestuous thing
That joy would lift, and sorrow would cast down;
Where faith would dwell, and hope and laughter spring;
Where love would have its kingdom and its crown.
I think God must have waited—awed to start
The mechanism of the human heart.

Against the heavy head-wind I would rise,
Borne up by its force, yet with something of my own power
Bearing me closer to the turquoise skies
Through wide and windy spaces, hour by hour.
The wings of my spirit strong against the might
That would deter me upon my upward way,
Above me the racing clouds, below, the white
Drift of the sea, its surge, its silver spray.

I would have gulls' wings on my heavenly climb,
I would be stronger than the winds that blow,
I would lift up beyond all space and time—
There is a haven for me—I would go
With wings against the wind, with wings widespread.
There is splendor above me, there is light ahead!

Here is such dark cool beauty, such clear sound:
An echo runs along the far-off heights
Like crystal striking crystal. Seaward bound
The mountain torrent, filled with silver lights,
Makes wild protest; and a trodden twig somewhere
Breaks, and the sound is loud upon the air.

An aspen quakes beside a waterfall.
The pines climb skyward, not a branch is stirred,
The blue spruce lifts against the canyon wall,
And now a dark bough dips where a crimson bird
With iridescent wings and breast of flame
Swings, and calls to his mate a singing name.

Deep in a dark cool tree a fiery bird
Has written a poem without pen or word.

How white the stars are in this inky blackness!
How strangely still the hills and hollows lie!
How cold beneath the passionless white fires
That burn like molten silver in the sky!
I am so small beneath their countless numbers,
So little and so lost in this vast dark,
I reach my hands to find some warmth and comfort
In fires a million light years off, each spark
Left smoldering from the white heat of creation:
Strange icy flames that have power to sear
Upon my heart how truly unimportant
Is this small earth, and man's brief sojourn here . . .
And yet, and yet—recalling God's great mercy
In sending Christ to tread this planet's sod,
I straighten in the starlight, I grow taller,
Remembering my significance to God.

The world is cleaner here than anywhere.
The stars are nearer here, and all the air
Is spangled with their splendor. I can stand
On tiptoe, almost touching with my hand
The silver fruit of heaven. I can see
The leaning orchards of eternity,
And God among the weighted shining trees
Feet-deep in silver globes. I think He sees
My upraised hands, my eager lifted eyes,
For suddenly from out the startled skies
One silver apple falls. Deliberately
God reached a hand and shook a nearby tree.
I am sure He loosed that starry fruit for me!

So many hearts are brave. Each day I see
The lifted banners of their courage shine.
Out of the myriad eyes that look in mine.

The banners mankind carry as they march
To prove that they are undefeated still
Though tired feet must often drag behind;
Though there be scarcely strength to climb the hill.
Brave women, and brave men, who go their way
Without the blare of music down the street;
Without the cheers, or the encouragement
Of words that would be heartening and sweet.

So many have the courage to go on
Undaunted by their loss, or pain or fear;
Beaten perhaps, yet holding in their souls
The beautiful bright quality of cheer.
So many hearts are brave—though well they know
How rough the road is that their feet must go.

An old man sat one evening by his door;
His face was tranquil, in his eyes was peace,
His hands were still, his long life work was done,
He had a look about him of release.

And I, who needed much to learn the things
That he had learned, sat down beside him there
On the low doorstep in the scented dusk;
He smiled his gentle smile, he touched my hair,
He said: "My child, I, too, was restless once;
I, too, was hurt by life, and blind and dumb
I groped my way; then a wise one said these words:
'If you are quiet, so will help come.'
'Twas an old folk saying from an old loved land.
I listened to its teaching, listened long,
And learned its secret: He who trusts in God,
And who goes quietly, he will grow strong."

O Blessed Lord, I stoop to Thy flowing garment,
I reach a timid hand to touch its hem
Here among the throng that is surging, pressing
Close about Thee, and I the humblest of them.
Then lo, He speaks, and His voice is kind and gentle:
"Who in this throng has touched me?" questions He;
And I, who have been needing it so, move forward
To receive the wondrous gift He is giving me:
The gift of healing for body, mind and spirit,
The gift of virtue from His own life to mine,
And He speaks the blessed words of commendation:
"Thy faith hath made thee whole." O words that shine
Like silver light to pierce the clouding darkness,
Humbly, indeed, I bow before that praise.
Grant me, O blessed One, the strength to follow
Thee closer—with greater faith throughout my days.

PRAYERS

Oh, God, the prayers that have gone up to Thee
To clutch Thy robes, to beat against Thy breast!
The hurt hearts crying out in agony,
The weary importuning Thee for rest;
The sad who seek to find Thee through their tears;
The glad who pray with lifted heart and light;
The patient who plead ceaselessly for years;
The craven kneeling down to Thee at night.

The whole world seeking One who understands.
A million prayers rise upward from the sod
Like smoking incense, and the lifted hands
Of kneeling multitudes beseech Thee, God.
If they would only listen as they seek—
Out of the silence they would hear Thee speak.

My being took on a brightness today that will last for-
ever:
I stood on a tip of the Great Divide whose high peaks sever
The East from the West, with all about me a blinding glory.
Stretching away as far as the eye could reach, the hoary
Heads of the mountains lifted, blurred in a violet vapor;
Far below in the running shadows of pines, an occasional
taper
Of a bare spruce caught the sun, and burned like an altar
fire;
A high lake cupped its holy water in, and a spire
Of rock gleamed with its cross of snow, while the wind came
bringing
An anthem where the joined voices of earth and sky were
singing.
And I stood there, caught up in a terrible dazzling white-
ness,
I cried aloud, and a cloud came down to cover the bright-
ness.

There is no variableness, there is no turning,
When Love sets out upon its long highroad,
Storms cannot bind it, nor the hills deter it;
These cannot keep it from its own abode.
Lustily it climbs the hills of morning;
Lustily it strides the valley loam.
Its feet are swift upon the slopes of evening
Taking its sure way home.

There is no variableness, there is no turning;
The song upon its lips remains the same,
Years cannot stifle it, nor the dust smother
The song, if love be worthy of the name.
Life cannot blind its eyes at all, nor dying
Blot out its poignant, clear remembering;
Love is a permanent, a bright insistence,
Love is a constant thing.

LET US KEEP CHRISTMAS

Whatever else be lost among the years
Let us keep Christmas still a shining thing;
Whatever doubts assail us, or what fears,
Let us hold close one day, remembering
Its poignant meaning for the hearts of men;
Let us get back our childlike faith again.

Wealth may have taken wings, yet still there are
Clear windowpanes to glow with candlelight;
There are boughs for garlands, and a tinsel star
To tip some little fir tree's lifted height.
There is no heart too heavy or too sad
But some small gift of love can make it glad.

And there are home-sweet rooms where laughter rings,
And we can sing the carols as of old.
Above the eastern hills a white star swings;
There is an ancient story to be told;
There are kind words and cheering words to say.
Let us be happy this glad Christ Child's day.

LEISURE

I shall attend to my little errands of love
Early this year,
That the brief days before Christmas may be
Unhampered and clear
Of the fever of hurry. The breathless rushing that I
Have known in the past
Shall not possess me; I shall be calm in my soul
And ready at last
For Christmas: "the Mass of the Christ." I shall kneel
And call out His name;
I shall take time to watch the beautiful light
Of a candle's flame;
I shall have leisure—I shall go out alone
From my roof and my door;
I shall not miss the silver silence of stars
As I have before,
And oh, perhaps, if I stand there very still,
And very long,
I shall hear what the clamor of living has kept from me:
The angels' song!

In all my life I never held
A water lily in my hand,
They lay so far beyond my reach
From where I stood upon the land.

But I have watched them, and have loved
Each little ivory-tinted boat:
The airy way they tilt and dip,
The light and windy way they float.

Pale barges, ready to set sail
To some far heavenly port of call.
They strain to leave their inlet ways
Where willows bend and reeds are tall.

If I could reach them, I would draw
Up all the frail green chains that hold
Them anchored, and would set them free
To sail their cargoes of pure gold.

I planted a rose and I talked with God
I looked straight into the high, bright blue
And I said, "Dear God, you do the rest,
I have done all that I can do."

The sun shone warm on the moist brown earth,
The wind from the south cooled my lifted face,
And I think God came from the far blue sky
To watch in my small sweet garden space.

For this morning I found it, the lovely thing:
A pink rose proud on its red-thorned stem,
And there, like little bright candles lit,
Were the pink-tipped buds, a score of them.

I believe God comes for a little while
When any new flower takes root and grows,
And I am quite sure that He comes and stays
When a woman prays as she plants a rose.

ART

The Japanese have known for long
That one flower in a slender vase
Is beautiful—and that one bright bough
Blowing against the sky, is grace;

And that a single lovely print
Upon a wall may rest the heart;
That there is quiet elegance
In simple things, and there is art.

We clutter up our hearts and minds;
We crowd our days and fail to see
How beautiful cleared spaces are;
How lovely some small thing may be.

LISTENING

Seek a cool green hilltop close to the sky
Where the unimpeded winds of heaven blow,
And the spread wings of wild birds whistle by,
Seeking some destination that they know.
Then close your eyes and listen . . . you will hear
The all but inaudible music at your feet
Of grasses that give forth a sound as clear
As tiny struck bells pealing true and sweet.
The impinging wings will make a silver sound
Brushing together as they lift and fly;
The wind's orchestral score will leap the ground
And run the gamut of the arching sky.
And you will find some gentle master hand
Turning the slack strings of your heart until
You come in harmony with this green land,
This cool, amazing, music-ridden hill.
You will hear the laughter and the sound of tears
Among old trees that have grown strangely wise—
You will hear voices no one ever hears
Unless he stands and listens with closed eyes.

WHO LOOKS AT BEAUTY

Who looks at beauty with glad eyes
And finds in it surcease from care,
Who marks each small and lovely thing,
Is praising God all unaware.

Whose heart lifts up in gratitude
For cloud and leaf and budding stem,
Is sharing the delight He knew
The morning He created them.

Whose ears are keened to catch the first
Faint bird note in the darkened trees,
Can hear the music of the spheres,
The ageless heavenly symphonies.

Who holds his breath at the far scent
Of some wild blossom on the air,
Is giving thanks unknowingly,
Is voicing an unspoken prayer.

CATHEDRAL WINDOW

This gorgeous colored window filled with light:
Purple and crimson, blue and green and white,
Its patterned kaleidoscopic jewels turned
To a perpetual loveliness, and burned
With opal, amethyst and emerald fire,
Catches the sun, runs ceiling high, and higher,
Until the dark cathedral walls are lit
With facet color, richly exquisite.

Outside at night it is a glowing thing:
A poem to be read, a song to sing,
A light to follow, and a prayer to pray;
It is a clear voice, calling men away
From darkness and despair to seek a place
Where they can kneel and meet God face to face.

Quick, for night is coming down the river!
Whistler could have held this, why not I?
Quick, my pencil, make slim alders quiver,
Stencil that frieze against the western sky;
Catch the sound of low wings whirring, wheeling,
The lip-lap of the water, the deep blur
Of mist and shadow—hold the breathless feeling
Of wet wind where the shore-lined willows stir!

Pencil, paint beneath deft, flying fingers,
That dim, high bridge, that wash of silent grays,
Make this moment, while the late light lingers,
A misty miracle of beauty for all days . . .
The dark, swift night has come, and I could cry!
Whistler could have held this, why not I?

ARTICULATION

When the curtains of the Blessed Country part
Some evening in the West to let me through,
A keen delight will quicken in my heart,
My faltering, slow tongue will speak with new
Articulation, and the words I seek
And long for now, will sparkle up in me
Like clear cold water and my lips will speak
A language fraught with strange intensity.

I shall have words for April twilights then;
For the look of autumn sunlight on a wall,
A thousand things the earth-bound tongues of men
Have tried to voice yet never speak at all,
And in some corner, quivering with delight,
I shall sit down and write—and write—and write.

Beautiful land of strange and magnificent distances,
Land of heartbreak and of wild exultant joy,
Spent from centuries of shock, yet holding within you
A heady virility that nothing can destroy.

No one has gathered unto themselves your wastelands,
Your wide gray spaces ridden by wind and sun;
Yours is an independence that none can conquer;
Though men may court you for years you will not be won.

You have borne no fruit at all, no vital yielding,
The kiss of the wind is all you have ever known.
O wild, strange, beautiful land—have you found that beauty
Is enough for your untamed living? Beauty alone?

I saw an eagle with a shattered wing
Fall on a rocky slope, and there he lay
Impotent, tense, a furious feathered thing
Of shock and fierce incredible dismay.
His eyes were circling fires of topaz light,
They burned the heavens with their piercing glare,
His great wings heaving, straining to take flight
Once more into the limitless blue air:

Those starry spaces that his splendid strength
Had bridged a thousand times; those chasmed walls
That knew his cries along their breadth and length,
And answered with their challenging, clear calls,
A comrade to the lightning and the rain,
The thunder's mate, the wind's own flying breath—
Humiliated, scornful of strange pain,
As proud as Lucifer . . . and done to death!

MARSHLAND DUSK

Dusk on the wide low land—
The mirrored water showing
Silver among the reeds
Where the whispering night winds roam,
The rush of black-winged bats,
And dark on the after glowing
The circling whir of wings
Where the herons are coming home.

Careening over the bogs
The hurrying birds are falling
Into their rush-lined nests
After their headlong flight;
The croak of a diving frog,
And a killdee's plaintive calling,
And the flush of the twilight lost
In the deepening blue of night.

Fluttering birds through the falling snow,
Softly their whirring wing-tips throw
A flurry of white flakes, shattering
Their tremulous slant, and scattering
A frost-dust as they wheel and light
Like feather flowers, dusky white
And slaty gray, and buff and brown,
Circling, swooping, coming down
A mist of color on the day,
A snow-veiled, heavenly bouquet
That falls and takes my breath away.

SEEKERS

They who earnestly set forth tonight
To seek the Highest shall not lose their way,
A star will go before them for a light;
The night's vast distances need not dismay;
Somewhere beyond the desert's farthest rim
They will come at last to Him.

He who zealously desires to find
The good in others need not know defeat,
For deep within the heart of all mankind
Is something brave and something clean and sweet;
Something of God and something of His Son
Is imaged in each one.

Let us be wise as the old wise men were wise;
Let us be seekers—coming from very far
Out of the dusk, surely at last our eyes
Shall see the silver wonder of His star
Surely we shall be guided by that light,
O comrades of the night.

THE UNTRAVERSED COUNTRIES

Within the human heart are many regions
Undreamed of, and still waiting to be found:
There are new paths to blaze in thought and action,
Far journeys to be made to higher ground.
In the undiscovered countries of our being
Are forces steeped with power; there is new
Wide knowledge to be gained through toil and study;
There is startling creative work to do,

So many strange resources to discover:
God-given graces that have gone unnamed,
High courage for some unexpected testing,
Prayer power that has not been fully claimed.
So many regions in us undiscovered,
Such possibilities within each breast!
The wealth of unmined jewels, heights unconquered
Await the seekers in this glorious quest.

No matter how dark the night, how deep the shadows,
Still up beyond the cloud's obscuring bars,
Steadfast and silent, safe within God's keeping,
Move the radiant, self-illumined stars.

So I shall face skyward though the blackness
Sheds not one ray of light upon the air.
I know that back of the overhanging darkness
The white unfailing stars are ever there,

Moving by God's remote control, and taking
Their clearly outlined courses, swift and free.
It comforts me to know that same great power
Controls my heart, my life, my destiny.

TRAVELERS

You who have turned the corner out of my sight,
You who are lost somewhere in the sunset light,
Shout from the distance, tell me what of the road?
What of the Inns where one can unloose his load?
What of the wayside springs? Are there trees for shade?
Are there clear-cut paths that other feet have made?
How did you find the way at the very end?
It would comfort me to hear from you, my friend.

And the answer is borne on the wind: "The road is long,
But none too steep for the heart that carries a song;
The noontime sun is hot, but there ever will be
The sheltering shade of a rock or a wayside tree.
The Inns are friendly, and always at some cool brink,
When water is needed, water is there to drink.
Comrade, take heart, forget your anxious care.
Whatever roads you must travel, God will be there."

YOUTH

Youth passed me by before I knew
That youth was sweet.
She tripped across the summer days
With dancing feet,
Her lithe young body slim and strong,
Her red lips parted with a song,
A girl with dusky, wind-blown hair,
My own youth lost somewhere.

How could I know that youth was sweet?
A world away
The white lights beckoned me to come,
None bade me stay,
The blue mist on the mountain height,
The rapturous silver stars at night,
The red enchantment of the dawn—
Everything—called me on.

I did not know that youth was sweet,
But now I know,
I watch them pass—young, star-eyed girls,
And love them so.
They do not see me as they pass
Their feet are swift upon the grass,
The far lights beckon them away—
And I—would bid them stay.

This is a thing that I remember
Crystal-clear from my girlhood days;
A sunset bell in a far, white steeple,
Calling the village to prayer and praise.

Over the fields came a peal of silver,
Sharp on the air as a bugle blown,
Setting the evening air aquiver,
With the sweetest notes I ever have known:

A mingle of sound and light and color—
A call like a voice down the sunset way,
And the village folk would stop their labor,
And pause for a little while to pray.

Sometimes now of a smoky evening,
Above the city's clamor and din,
I think that I surely catch the echo
Of a sunset bell pealing high and thin.

But no one stops for a breathless moment,
And no one prays at the far, sweet call—
I wonder . . . perhaps I am mistaken,
And it was not a bell that I heard, at all.

When I went down to Avonlee
The air was gold as honey,
My feet were light as thistledown,
My purse was full of money.

So many shining things to buy
Before the day was ended:
A length of silk, a pair of shoes
No cobbler's hand had mended.

A trinket for my wayward hair,
A new much-needed bonnet,
And it must have a crimson rose,
And a bow of velvet on it . . .

But somewhere on the road I lost
My purse—and could not find it!
I wept, then told my heart it was
A foolish thing to mind it.

And I went home at evening time,
The new moon sailing over,
The dew all wet upon the grass,
The twilight sweet with clover,

And every little house I passed
Sent up a curling feather,
Where there were women making tea,
And families were together.

Quite empty-handed, home I came,
But I am rich recalling
The morning walk to Avonlee,
And back when night was falling.

DUFFY'S WOOD

I have not been to Duffy's wood
For such a long, long while,
But still it lies somewhere beyond
A long lane and a stile.

Sweet Williams and May-apple blooms
Still glimmer back at me:
The scent of pennyroyal lifts
Near every rooted tree.

Each sunny autumn day I catch
The scent of hickory smoke;
I hear the old wood wagon creak
In every turning spoke.

And oh, the rattle of the nuts
That strike the leaf-strewn ground!
In all the world there never is
A cleaner, crisper sound.

I have not been to Duffy's wood
For years . . . I lost the track.
I followed down another road
And never shall get back.

Strange that a slender withe can hold
Within its silken thread a thing
So poignant, that a willow tree
Beside a stream has power to bring
One far-off May day back again,
Where a boy with a whittling, tapping blade
Shapes a whistle, and gives a girl
The exquisite gift that his hands have made.

And there on a windy hill they stand,
The wild flowers tossing about their feet,
A whistle between the girl's red lips,
And a sudden high note, shrill and sweet,
Pierces the air as a bird takes wing
Swift as the wind . . . Oh, I never see
A willow fringing a stream in spring
But that May morning comes back to me.

We leaned from our high window looking down
Over the mooned-white roofs of the island town,
And you said: "This is a thing to remember and to hold,
This is one of earth's splendors . . ." The clear gold
Of moonlight lit a wide and glittering track
Across the sea, the tall fringed palms were black,
The bougainvillea caught the misty light
And shimmered on their trellises, the night
Smoldered and glowed with dark hibiscus fires.
Each with its cross the old cathedral spires
Burned with beauty—roof and ivied wall
Drenched with molten silver, and the tall
Arched windows, stained with colored paint
Reflected dimly many a pictured Saint.

"A thing to remember," you said, "a lifetime through—
One of earth's splendors . . ." Ah, how well you knew!

I HAVE FORGOTTEN

I have forgotten other days that held
Distress like this, and grief, and baffling pain;
Perhaps I shall forget this bitter day
And not remember it again.

I trust it may be lost among the years,
As lost as one flake in a falling snow;
As lost as some persistent pleading voice
That has ceased speaking long ago.

Surely, my heart, among the coming years
The days will bring us laughter for a guest,
And gladness will companion us, and peace
Will be our portion, and our rest.

From dawn to dusk the old sun takes its way
And leaves no imprint on the sky's blue arc—
God grant this long heartbreaking day will pass
Into forgetfulness—and leave no mark.

A PRAYER FOR INNER STRENGTH

I know somehow that time will heal this sorrow,
This bitter grief, and that the years will bring
Forgetfulness and peace, that some tomorrow
Will hold no memory of my suffering.
And I believe that there will be a blurring
Of the jagged edges of the wounds I bear,
And in my heart again will be the stirring
Of laughter that has long been absent there.

I know all this, yet still cannot remember . . .
I cannot see beyond this wall of tears . . .
Yet as the falling ashes cool an ember,
So will my heart find comfort through the years.
I know—but God, dear God, my need is great!
Give me the inner strength this day to wait.

This, too, will pass. Oh, heart, say it over and over
Out of your deepest sorrow, out of your grief,
No hurt can last forever, perhaps tomorrow
Will bring relief.

This, too, will pass. It will spend itself, its fury
Will die as the wind dies down at the set of sun;
Assuaged and calm you may rest at last, forgetting
A thing that is done.

Repeat it again and again, oh, heart, for your comfort:
This, too, will pass, as surely as passed before
The old forgotten pain and the other sorrows
That once you bore.

As certain as stars at night or dawn after darkness,
Inherent as the lift of the blowing grass,
Whatever your despair or your frustration—
This, too, will pass.

There have been days of anguish, nights of pain,
The heart has ached, the way has not been clear;
But I shall take life by the hand once more
And by God's grace I shall go on from here.
Though I must journey for a while alone
Since the hand I held in mine has loosed its hold,
I shall go on a way I have not known
Through summer's heat and through the winter's cold.

But an unseen Presence will be there to stay
My stumbling feet and give me power to stand.
I shall have His promised strength for every day,
As I move out across an untrod land.
I shall not falter and I shall not fear.
God helping me, I shall go on from here.

THE HARPIST

His harp in his hands, there in the windy grasses,
Youthful David plucked out on its golden strings
Beautiful running music as clear as spring water,
Sweet as a bird's song, soft as impinging wings.
Nearby was the wind in the grass that he must capture
And there was the sound of water over stones;
There were the shadows racing along the hilltops
All to be translated to golden tones.

There were the fruitful trees and there were the cedars
As filled with music as sunlight fills new leaves—
And the eager youth must find a way to hold it;
He must capture the glinting light on the harvest sheaves.
And he must sing the songs that were ever surging
Like the waves of the sea within his boyish breast:
Songs beyond himself of the great Jehovah,
Strange new songs that never would let him rest.

We are the city dwellers, you and I,
And we would meet, oh, often if we could;
But tangled streets and walls flung on the sky
Have separated us, you who are good
And true, and I who love you. Days go fast,
And though I miss you much, I seldom see
Your face, or you see mine, as the years fly past,
The city throbbing between us ceaselessly.

If we lived on a prairie, you and I,
With this same distance that divides us here,
It would be nothing there, the friendly sky
Would tuck our little houses in, my dear,
And out across the miles a path would go—
Seeking each other, we would follow it,
And every night our casement lamps would glow,
Cheerful and warm for each when they were lit.

Outside the city thunders, but in here
Are cool deep aisles of silence where men look
With eager eyes to find some wonder-book
Throbbing with light and beauty . . . tier on tier
Of crowded shelves lift their abundant store
For those who seek with swift devouring eyes,
Adventure, Romance, Truth, to make them wise.
But in a separate space beside the door,
A man with searching finger stoops to find
A title, feeling with those sensitive quick tips
Along the shelf, and pausing at a book:
One of the few here written for the blind,
He clutches it—a smile upon his lips,
And on his face a pleased and radiant look.

The music of the wind through blowing grasses,
The song the wild birds sang for him alone,
The echoes floating back from far-off passes,
David, the shepherd, claimed and made his own.
His harp strings caught the wind—its golden singing
Was rapture to his heart; his mind, adream,
Captured the rhythmic sound of willows swinging
Their delicate fronds upon the meadow stream.

His sensitive fingertips set music flying,
Weighted with laughter, jeweled with clear light,
And through the minor strains, the lonely crying
Of storm-tossed cedars, of lost lambs at night . . .
Those same deft fingers that would soon release
A small brook stone to bring a nation peace.

A moment is but one quick breath,
An hour, one small golden while,
A day, a space from dawn to dusk,
The clock's hands move about the dial,
And it is night. God only gives
The promised strength from day to day.
Within this small enclosure He
Has placed us, and He bids us stay.

Standing between these two eternities:
The Past and Present, now, this very hour,
Ah, wise indeed is he whose clear eyes see
A moment's vast importance, and the power
Within him for fine living, as the brief
Swift present flows with scarce a shadow cast,
Forever backward, swift beyond belief,
Running like some bright stream into the past.

The future rushes toward us . . .   O my heart,
Lay hold upon this moment, it alone
Is all of time in which we have a part,
Is all of life that we can call our own.
Clasp beauty close, hold truth, lest they take wing,
Thus make this brief swift while a shining thing.

God, make me brave for life,
Oh, braver than this!
Let me straighten after pain
As a tree straightens after the rain,
Shining and lovely again.

God, make me brave for life,
Much braver than this!
As the blown grass lifts let me rise
From sorrow with quiet eyes,
Knowing Thy way is wise.

God, make me brave. Life brings
Such blinding things.
Help me to keep my sight,
Help me to see aright,
That out of the dark comes light.

THE MIRACLE

The pain has ceased! O heart, somewhere
We met the Master on the way.
It may be that we marked Him not
Amid the multitude today;
But it was Jesus, for behold
The old, old pain is gone, and, lo!
A miracle, no less than that
Upon the road to Jericho!
No less, my heart, we leapt to meet
The joy His healing fingers hold,
Than he who caught the glad sweet light
Across Judea's hills of old.

Ah, Master, Thou whose love still keeps
Thee pitiful, I bow to Thee.
My wistful, tired heart is filled
With this strange, wondrous ecstasy.
I thank Thee that we still can find
Thee close along the old earth-way;
That risen, yet somehow, somewhere,
We met Thee on the road today.

COMPENSATION

I cried when Pain took my laughter,
My joy, and my ecstasy,
And I fainted the night that Sorrow
Made his abode with me.

Today a white flower blossomed
Down the worn path Pain had trod,
And out of my sorrow walked one
Like unto the Son of God.

How can he thank Thee, Lord, for the good grain
Who has not conquered thistle and briar and weed?
How can he thank Thee for the sweet wild rain
Who has not trod parched lands above dead seed?
How can he lift a grateful heart for peace
Who has not known some red-lit battlefield?
O Lord, how can he comprehend release
Who has not felt at last an old wound healed?

Out of earth's agony white flowers shine;
Above old scarred fields wild grasses run;
Out of the crushed fruits of the sun comes wine,
Out of the night—the morning star—the sun.
For every hour of pain that we have had—
Even for these—Lord help us to be glad.

UPON LOOKING AT HOFFMAN'S PICTURED CHRIST

I am indebted to you, who have given
A concrete form, a gracious lovely face
To Him, our Christ. So often I have striven
To picture Him myself, His simple grace,
His form, His eyes, His hair—its haloed light,
And I could never visualize Him, quite.

But as you give Him to us, always there,
Captured by your magic brush, I see
His power, His might, His gentleness, His care,
His love, miraculously held for me;
Your interpretation has sufficed
To show me a divine, yet human Christ.

SOMEONE HAD PRAYED

The day was long, the burden I had borne
Seemed heavier than I could longer bear,
And then it lifted, but I did not know
Someone had knelt in prayer.

Had taken me to God that very hour,
And asked the easing of the load, and He,
In infinite compassion, had stooped down
And taken it from me.

We cannot tell how often as we pray
For some hurt one, bewildered and distressed,
The answer comes—but many times those hearts
Find sudden peace and rest.

Someone had prayed, and Faith, a reaching hand,
Took hold of God, and brought Him down that day!
So many, many hearts have need of prayer—
Oh, let us pray!

THE ENDURING THINGS

I will lay hold upon enduring things.
I am wearied with the din and noise and fret.
About me close, distracting, meager things
Grapple my soul—Lord, help me to forget
The clamor of it. Grant me peace that stills,
Deep peace of quietness, and hope that cheers.
I lift my eyes to Thy strength-giving hills,
Steeped in the light of far eternal years.

I will lay hold upon enduring things:
Faith that illumines though the eyes be blind,
And joy continuous, a heart that sings,
And love that suffers long—yet still is kind.
They are such paltry things I've bartered for,
I am soul-sick with the weariness it brings.
Now—with high-lifted face I turn me, for
I will lay hold upon enduring things.

My Lord, I pray that through today
I may walk patiently,
Forgetting not that Thy dear hand
Is leading me.

I know not what Thy wisdom, Lord,
May choose for me today;
What the long hours may hold for me
I cannot say.

I only know that I may go
Unquestioningly with Thee,
Remembering that what Thou wilt
Is best for me.

For Thou, O Lord, canst see the end,
While I but see the way—
Help me to walk it patiently
Throughout today.

FIRST FROST

"There will be frost," my mother used to say
When an evening came, and the gusty wind would die.
We would stand and watch our garden as it lay
Bathed in the clear cold light from the western sky.
The few remaining asters caught the glow
And held it as one holds cold hands to fire;
The lovely dahlias, that so soon must go,
Seemed standing with their proud heads even higher.
The marigolds, we thought, would bear the frost,
Their brilliant orange warming them like flame,
But oh, to see that other beauty lost
Filled me with a grief that had no name!
I longed to start a fire beside each root,
To fling my body down to shelter them.
The morning would find the blossoms turned to soot,
A brittle blackness numbing every stem . . .
The air was clear and cold and crystal-thin—
I ran out, cut them all, and brought them in.

I took my little braided rug
And laid it by the fire;
I drew two chairs beside the hearth
And piled the dry wood higher;
The kettle started singing out,
The cat began her purring,
No other sound was in the room
Except the small clock's whirring.
It struck the hour and then was still,
The room was sweet and quiet;
I was so glad my fire burned
And I was sitting by it;
I was so glad the sun shone in,
And that I had one flower;
A little scarlet spray of light
To brighten that good hour.
The other chair was empty quite,
No one came in—and only
The kettle, cat, and I were there
But still I was not lonely.
My mind ran bright with happiness
As glowing as an ember . . .
Strange, how the heart will choose one hour
From many, to remember!

Why should I long for other lands?
Why should I care to roam?
I can find the same skies over me,
The same green hills at home,
The same old earth beneath my feet,
The same moon sheds its light
Above my roof as that which floods
The Appian Way tonight.

The wild flowers down my country road
Yield perfume quite as sweet
As the costliest attars—why should I
Have restless hands and feet,
When the humanity surrounding me,
Of which I am a part,
Differs so very little from
The old-world folk at heart?

136

THE TIN PEDDLER

He used to come with a rattle and din
Up the long lane to our farmhouse door:
A gay Adventurer, dealing in tin,
And exciting indeed was his shining store
Of pans and buckets and tubs locked tight
In his strong box built on his wagon bed,
And he had seen many a wondrous sight,
For he had been everywhere, he said.

He would stay for dinner and in exchange
Would trade his wares with a quip and a grin:
A kettle to set on our kitchen stove,
Or a sieve or a funnel of soldered tin.
He usually managed some sale for cash.
"I need the money, and live I must,"
He would say, then mount, and his whip's sharp lash
Would start him off in a flurry of dust.

And we children would watch with a light in our eyes
From the dazzle of new tin flashed in the sun.
Oh, the vanishing one was brave and wise,
And sorry we were when his visit was done.
The peddler has gone down the long, long road,
And gone are the children who watched him there
Wheeling away with his shining load
Into the world's far Everywhere . . .
If ever you meet him, tell him, pray,
That I'm needing some of his wares today!

Looking back along the years
I can see the hand of God
Leading me down every road
That my feet have trod.

I can see the long steep hills
That I dreaded so to climb,
Now I know He went with me
Up them every time.

And I find He walked with me
When I thought I walked alone
Through those far-off, shadowed, dark
Valleys I have known.

So today why should I doubt,
And today why should I fear?
Sometime I shall look and see
Even now, God near.

NIGHT

Thank God for night, with its great gift of sleep:
More wonderful than all His gifts to men!
For stars that walk the dreamways, and that keep
Their wide-eyed watch until dawn breaks again.
Thank God for blessed silence down the land:
More soothing than the drip of summer rain;
For darkness, soft and cool as some dear hand
Laid on a forehead, feverish with pain.

Oh, only those who carry sleepless scars,
Can know how sweet sleep is that comes at last;
And only the eyes that have looked long at stars,
Have learned night's secret as it marches past;
Have learned to know how quiet God must keep
To guide an earth through stars that men may sleep.

TRANQUILITY

It should not be so difficult to find
The long way back, O Heart, if we but turn
Down the dim road that we have left behind,
And cross the old stile where the maples burn
Like lifted torches on the smoky air;
It cannot be so very far from there . . .

And we may find again that lost delight:
A field's dark furrows bronzed with evening sun;
May see the first star shyly come in sight,
The first star lighted when the day is done;
May hear a lonely cricket sing a song
That we once knew and have not heard for long.

Surely there still is peace in sky and ground—
O Heart, if we but search, it can be found!

The field is worn from yielding the good grain.
Fallow it lies, its furrows dark and still.
Beneath the blinding sun and bitter rain
It patiently awaits its master's will.
It draws new power as the year goes by
From winds that sweep across its furrowed way;
It pulls the sunlight from the bending sky,
And holds it there to use again some day.

Now I, like any barren field, must lie
Fallow awhile. God make me wise to wait
As old fields do through storms, nor question why
Strength comes so slowly, peace so very late.
Let me draw power from this time, and then,
Strengthened anew, rise up to serve again.

HOPE

This would I hold more precious than fine gold,
This would I keep although all else be lost:
Hope in the heart, that precious, priceless thing,
Hope at any cost.

And God, if its fine luster should be dimmed,
If seemingly through grief it may be spent,
Help me to wait without too much despair,
Too great astonishment.

Let me be patient when my spirit lacks
Its high exuberance, its shining wealth;
Hope is a matter, often, God, I know
Of strength, of health.

Help me to wait until my strength returns,
Help me to climb each difficult high slope,
Always within my heart some golden gleam,
Some quenchless spark of hope.

SPRING FRESHET

I like the look of snow when it is melting
And sending its clear rivulets toward the sea;
I like the sweep of dry grasses bending
Beneath those bright feet, suddenly set free.

I have seen small green leaves under water
That snow had hidden through the winter hours,
Fresher and greener and sweeter than the leafing
That springs to life after the April showers:

A little clover leaf washed clean by waiting,
Eager for life again at the hint of spring!
I reach my fingers into the icy water
To touch that tender, tremulous, wistful thing,

Knowing a kinship with it, deep and abiding,
I, too, have waited until the winter passed,
And I lift my head after a strange chastisement
To the bright air again, the sun at last!

Lord, it is dark, the road is rough to go;
I lift an unlit candle in the night,
Behold it, Lord, within my upraised hand;
Touch it to flame with Thine own heavenly light.

This slender waxen thing that is my faith,
Fire it, Lord, with some divine white spark,
Until its circle, widening at my feet,
Will mark my certain way across the dark.

"Thou wilt light my candle" . . . thus assured
I shall go forward through this unknown land;
The way can never grow too dark, too long,
For I shall bear Thy light within my hand.

I have learned these things by the light of the years
Like a child conning over his books,
That the darkness outside of my window at night
Is never as dark as it looks,
And if I but run out and search, I can find
Some little light, steady and kind.

I have learned that Hope is the white feathered bird
That sings all day in my breast;
That Fear is the crouching beast that comes
To tear the bird from its nest.
I heave learned to close the door on Fear
After many and many a year.

I have patiently learned that Pain will cease
Tho' peace comes slowly and late,
And that there will drift down to sleepless eyes
Lost sleep at last, if I wait,
So why should I worry and fret and cry,
Knowing these things pass by.

I have learned that to doubt is to hurt One who long
Has walked by my side and been true;
That Faith wears a shining face, and to trust
Is the grateful, wise thing to do.
I have studied it long by the light of the years,
And have learned it through my tears.

ANTIQUES

Antiques? Some woman did not deem them so!
They were modern to her long ago, and new.
That whatnot, chair, and table in this show,
Clearly depict what time alone can do.
That far-off day she set them in their place
They shone with newness: walnut, glass, and plush,
Her china figurines were things of grace,
Her velvet carpets, flower-sprigged and lush.

Now in this dusty shop they wait apart,
Battered, yet repaired ingeniously,
Set to delight some antique-seeker's heart.
She would weep today, I know, if she could see
Her once new treasures ready to be sold
Holding the mute appeal of things grown old.

OLD PRINTS

I turn this sheaf of yellowed prints and see
Our America of another century:
The march of time depicted clear and true,
The joys and sorrows that a people knew
Who filled the village streets or tramped the roads;
Their customs, their inventions and abodes
Are captured in these lithographs, their lives
Kept chronicled by Currier and Ives.

Hung upon countless walls of other days
Romantic lovers went, robe-wrapped in sleighs.
The drunkard's downfall has been plainly shown,
The hunter faced his fighting foe alone,
The fire engines puffed their smoky way,
The sinking ships went down in crashing spray,
Prim men and women skated in the park,
A darkened parlor—where two lovers spark,
Their quarrels, their reconciliations told . . .
A million of these quaint old prints were sold,
Were loved, and then discarded for a while,
Grown so old-fashioned, they provoked a smile.
Today, collectors, spending without stint
Are glad to pay small fortunes for one print.

To understand how lengthened time must be
Since the world began—look on a stormy sea:
Its gray face furrowed by the plows of care,
Its foaming beard atoss, its thinned white hair
Whipped by the wind—pale light-revealing eyes
Lost to any wonder or surprise.
Worn with tumult, saddened by the years,
Its hollow cheeks adrip with salty tears,
It is as old as time itself—this wandering Jew
Whose troubled voyaging is never through.

Look on a stormy sea if you would know
Of ages far away and long ago.

If I can put new hope within the heart
Of one who has lost hope,
If I can help a brother up
Some difficult long slope
That seems too steep for tired feet to go,
If I can help him climb
Into the light upon the hill's far crest,
I shall begrudge no time
Or strength that I can spend, for well I know
How great may be his need.
If I can help through any darkened hour,
I shall be glad indeed.

For I recall how often I have been
Distressed, distraught, dismayed,
And hands have reached to help, and voices called
That kept me unafraid.
If I can share this help that I have had,
God knows I shall be glad.

It has taken long for me to learn
The simple lessons that the Master taught:
To consider the lilies as their petals burn
Among the wayside grasses, to take no thought
Of a tomorrow that may never bring
Some direful, long-anticipated thing;
To mark the sparrows on a windy stem
Lashing and dipping in a day of storm,
And to remember that He cares for them,
And shelters them and keeps them from all harm;
And that I am more valuable than they
To Him who walks beside me day by day.

"Let not your heart be troubled . . ."—these His words
Should have been learned and heeded long ago.
I should have lived lighthearted as the birds;
I should have marked the lilies— Ah, too slow
Has been my heart in learning how to live.
Dear God, You tried to teach me. Please forgive.

TOMORROW'S BRIDGE

Tomorrow's bridge as I look ahead
Is a rickety thing to view:
Its piers are crumbled, its rails are down,
Its floor would let me through.

The chasm it spans is dark and deep,
And the waters foam and fret;
I have crossed that bridge a thousand times
Though I never have reached it yet.

It has crashed beneath me to let me through,
Although it is miles away;
But strange, the bridges that I have crossed
Have all been safe today.

Perhaps I shall find when I reach that one
That lies in the distant blue,
Some hand may have mended its rickety floor
And its piers may be strong and new.

And I can pass over, lighthearted, free,
As a bird on the buoyant air—
Forgive me, God, for my fearful heart,
My anxious and foolish care.

How deaf we are! The music of the spheres
Still rolls upon its far eternal way;
The voices we have loved and lost for years
Are sounding on the ether waves today;
The spoken words of Christ are echoing back
Like clear-struck bells along the aerial track.

How blind we are! About us all the air
Is luminous with wings. Above earth's sod
Is constant light and motion everywhere
As white souls take their flaming way to God,
And infant spirits ever flutter down
Like autumn's bright leaves falling on a town.

The cattle are no dumber. God, unbind
Our ears, our eyes, that are so deaf and blind.

If we could see beyond a present sorrow,
Beyond a present grief, as God can see,
We would be braver, knowing some tomorrow
Will still hold happiness for you and me.

If our blurred eyes could glimpse beyond their weeping,
The sunlit hills that someday we shall climb,
We would be stronger, and we would be keeping
A tryst with Hope through every darkened time.

If we could see beyond a fresh disaster,
The road smoothed out again before our eyes,
We would be calmer, and we would learn faster
The lessons life unfolds to make us wise.

We are so blinded by a moment's grieving,
So hurt by any sorrow, any pain,
That we forget the joys, beyond believing,
The peace that someday will be ours again.

Because someone has faith in me
I cannot fail though all the way
Winds up the hill.
My staff in hand, and cheerily,
I can but fare me forth each day
With right good will.

Because someone has faith in me
I need to keep my heart quite true,
My own faith strong,
My vision clear, that I may see,
Undaunted by what meets my view,
And sing a song.

God help me sing the song, I pray,
God keep me clean and strong to go,
Clear-eyed to see
The untrod, upward-winding way,
For fail I cannot; one I know
Has faith in me.

God keep a clean wind blowing through my heart,
Night and day,
Cleanse it with sunlight, let the silver rain
Wash away
Cobwebs, and the smoldering dust that years
Leave, I pray.

God keep a clean wind blowing through my heart:
Wind from far
Green pastures, and from shaded pools where still
Waters are;
Wind from spaces out beyond the first
Twilight star.

Bitterness can have no place in me,
Nor grief stay,
When the winds of God rush through and sweep
Them away.
God keep a clean wind blowing through my heart
Night and day.

This is no ordinary wood and fire,
These dark still faggots with their restless flame,
Their brilliant colors ever straining higher
As if to seek some lost way that they came.
Swift wave on wave of splendor rolling in
Against my blackened hearth to speak to me
In a strange tongue of journeys they have been
To gather the deep secrets of the sea,
The phosphorescent sea whose waters break
Against far tropic isles, bleak northern shores.
Out of its darkened heart the driftwood takes
Its brilliant hues, its ocean-gathered stores,
And in one burst of beauty leaps and cries
Its hidden secrets as it fades and dies.

Long centuries ago it stood—a wonder-thing:
A tree, pregnant with the voices of the rains and seas,
Swept with the passion of the wind's wild melodies,
Bowed with the grief of storms, and stilled to slumbering,
Drenched with white moon showers, and called upon to sing
Songs of old loves, old dreams, and deep desires,
Told in the rose of dawn, and sunset's scarlet fires:
Songs of the rapturous spheres, too sweet for uttering.

Then came an hour—the axe, the shrieking fall,
The travail—and a violin drew breath
To sigh and sob and sing of life and death:
A glorious interpreter of all
Dreams, delight, despair, that holds for me
Heartbreak, beauty, and a strange wild ecstasy.

Throughout the ages men have ever clung
To the everlasting promises of God.
When loss and grief and suffering have wrung
Their hearts, the pilgrims journeying on earth's sod
Have turned their faces skyward, and will turn
Forever toward the arching starlit skies,
Where steadfastly His silver fires burn
Like words of flame before their seeking eyes.

O men, behold! Lift up your eyes and see
Who hath created them. He brings them out,
He names each one—He knows their destiny.
Not one will fail! Oh, we so prone to doubt,
Can we not trust the One through life's brief hour,
Who has such infinite, unfailing power?

I have seen such trust through deep distress,
Such shining faith when roadways have been dark,
Such valiant courage that the memories bless
My life like music. I have caught a spark
From that high flame and held it to my own
Small candle's wick until a sudden light,
Brighter than anything I then had known,
Kindled and lit my way across the night.

So for the sake of others I shall hold
My candle high—perhaps it, too, may shed
A little radiant spark of flying gold
To light some blackened wick that long was dead.
God, from Thy central powerhouse on high
Bid that no flame of faith may ever die.

So long I have been guided by Thy power
Up many a tangled path and stony hill,
And now, dear Lord, through this strange darkened hour
Be with me still.

Be with me, for the way is long and lonely,
I am bewildered, and I cannot see,
But, Lord, I shall not be afraid if only
You walk with me.

If I can ever keep recalling
The darkened roads I traveled in the past,
How, after You long guarded me from falling,
Light shone at last:

Then surely, Lord, I can go forward knowing
That somewhere on the hills the light will dawn,
And I shall reach it safely if, in going,
You still lead on.

Still your hurrying heart, O journeying pilgrim,
Forging ahead beneath a burdening load.
You often may be weary, worn, and restless,
And feel there is no ending to the road;
But there are wayside pools by which to rest you,
And there is shade from many a greening tree.
There will be cold spring water for your thirsting
And glorious vistas for your eyes to see.

No doubt the journey's ending will be better
Than at the dawn or in the noontime heat.
Take heart. Look up—the hills ahead are golden;
The climb will be made easy for your feet.
And there upon the highest crest the sunset
Will point the way ahead with fingered flame,
And looking backward on the crimsoned lowlands
You will note the road was bright by which you came.

The frost came early those November nights,
The cornstalks withered, and the hills took fire
From the gold and scarlet of the autumn lights
That burned through painted leaves like fierce desire.
A partridge drummed, a fox-bark rent the air,
The stockade gates were shut, and none too soon,
The night in that strange region was a lair
For all wild things—the golden harvest moon
Climbed slowly upward . . . "We shall choose," they said,
"A special day to render thanks to God."
So on the morrow they had richly spread
Their tables with the good fruits of the sod.

"For these we offer thanks," a voice rang out,
A voice whose echo never has been spent.
Within the new land it became a shout—
A settlement became a Continent;
And men still offer thanks, and pause to pray
As the pilgrims did that first Thanksgiving Day.

Its eternal price is eternal vigilance,
And faith that sees the worth in any man;
The knowledge that no good thing comes by chance,
But must be labored for. Since time began
The struggle has been bitter, hard and long
To keep a principle intact and whole,
As mankind sought to shield from hurt and wrong
The priceless freedom of the human soul.

Hardships were there, and rough the frontiers crossed,
And blood was spilled upon embattled sod,
That men's religious freedom not be lost,
As conscientiously they worshiped God.
O men, keep faith! Fight ever valiantly
That this great basic freedom be kept free!

Sometimes, across this land of silver grasses,
There comes a sound upon the listening air
As if, along the old dim trails and passes,
Horses were there,
Galloping swiftly, riderless, unbidden,
Their smoky manes a blur against the light,
Wild horses that have never yet been ridden,
Lunging in fright
Before some scent or sound, some windward gleaning
Of distant threat, their arching necks held high,
Their ears alert to catch the inner meaning
Of step or cry . . .

Almost I see them down the windy weather,
Their satin muscles rippling as they run,
Wild horses that have never known a tether,
Mates to the sun,
Mates to the lightning and the crashing thunder,
The black-winged night, the white onrushing dawn—
Wild horses— Ah, the beauty and the wonder
Of things long gone!

PROMISES

The year will keep its promises to me:
Unfailingly the days will come and go;
Rivers will take their sure course to the sea;
Seedtime and harvest, these will come, I know.
The stars will go their quiet silver way;
There will be sun and rain and wind and dew;
There will be breathless beauty in each day;
There will be old loved tasks for me to do.

And I have made my promise to the year
(God help me keep it through the hours ahead):
I shall be braver, I shall banish fear;
I shall not leave a kindly word unsaid;
I shall have faith that this, my ancient grief,
Will yield at last to laughter and to song;
I shall have hope that there will be relief
For the old hurts the world has borne so long.

The year will keep its promise. Oh my heart,
We must not, dare not fail to do our part.

HIGH WIND

Something native to me in a high wind blowing
Makes me its comrade as it rides the earth.
I have been one with it in its speedy going,
I have been the wind's friend ever since my birth.

Restless and wild it is, scorning leash or tether:
The high wind sweeping out across the land and sea,
A bright wind, a dark wind, according to the weather—
Any wind swift enough is the wind for me.

Take me with you, bear me up, I, too, would be faring
On wind-wings as swift and free as the wild birds fly,
I who am your comrade, wind, surely would be sharing
Your unimpeded journey to the farthest sky.

WILD CHERRY

It is evening now, the early lamps are lighted,
The dusk is deep on street and city lot,
And at last the mind has leisure to remember
The things it once knew and long since forgot.

Strange that the dusk can hold as bright a picture
Of morning light on an old wild cherry tree
That stood alone in a far-off northern pasture,
And strange it has such perpetuity.

Silver the leaves as castanets in action,
Purple the fruit as grapes at harvest time,
The taste to the mouth like bitter wild-weed honey,
A tree too large to shake, too tall to climb.

We slaked our thirst for beauty, looking upward,
We fed our hunger at a tree's dark root;
And it still stands in bright perpetual summer,
And, years away, I feed upon its fruit.

Once in a dark and troubled time
When I saw no road ahead,
A wise and a kindly counselor
Sat by my side and said:
"Each morning I drive down a valley road
To get to my work, and I
Can often see nothing at all for the fog
That blots out the earth and sky;
But I say to myself, "I shall drive ahead,
Carefully, without sight.
For I know I shall come onto higher ground
Where the hills are gold with light.
And I just keep on . . ."
Oh, wise kind words
That fell on my heart that day,
Nothing can blot them from my mind,
Nothing can take them away,
And now when a thick fog shuts me in
To choke me and blind my eyes,
I am so glad for the hills ahead,
For the friend who was kind and wise!

I never came to you, my friend,
And went away without
Some new enrichment of the heart:
More faith, and less of doubt,
More courage for the days ahead,
And often in great need
Coming to you, I went away
Comforted, indeed.

How can I find the shining words,
The glowing phrase that tells
All that your love has meant to me,
All that your friendship spells?
There is no word, no phrase for you
On whom I so depend
All I can say to you is this:
God bless you, precious friend.

Whatever else be told of these years,
Or written, when they are past,
When out of the fog and the dark and the mire
We struggle at last,
This be said of the common folk,
This be said of them then:
They were brave, they were brave as they went their way,
These women and men.

This be said of them, this be told,
When the stress and the strain are done:
They faced their fears, and they lived their days,
They fought and they won;
They kept their love, and they kept their faith,
Their laughter followed their tears;
They were brave, they were brave, the common folk,
Through the dark years.

They draw me to them: women who have grown
Wise with the wisdom that right living brings.
Old mothers who have suffered and have known
A triumph over many conquered things.
Who have grown gentle, trusting day by day,
Who have grown patient, serving through the years;
Who, having prayed much, have learned how to pray,
And weeping—learned how futile were their tears.

They wear such certainty within their eyes:
A sureness that no questioning can shake;
All is so clear to them—they are so wise,
The way was made so plain that they should take.
If one should come to them—his faith grown dim—
Their faith would light the fires anew in him.

I THINK THAT GOD IS PROUD

I think that God is proud of those who bear
A sorrow bravely—proud indeed of them
Who walk straight through the dark to find Him there
And kneel in faith to touch His garment's hem.
Oh, proud of them who lift their heads to shake
Away the tears from eyes that have grown dim,
Who tighten quivering lips and turn to take
The only road they know that leads to Him.

How proud He must be of them—He who knows
All sorrow, and how hard grief is to bear!
I think He sees them coming, and He goes
With outstretched arms and hands to meet them there,
And with a look, a touch on hand or head,
Each finds his hurt heart strangely comforted.

172

THE IMPERATIVE PEACE

It is imperative that men find peace.
Even the whirlwind has a quietness
Deep in its heart where the wild, dark swirlings cease:
A center that is strangely motionless.
So in the awful clamor of these days
The heart must find a stillness all its own,
Must seek unfrequented and ancient ways
That the prophets and the sages long have known.

Go out, O Heart, beneath the star-filled skies;
Mark their calm journeyings, then seek a wood
Where only the winds are vocal; lift your eyes
And watch a tall tree's quiet certitude—
And you will find, whatever be the strife,
A central calmness settling in your life.

HORSE AND WAGON DAYS

I am lonely for the sound of wagon wheels,
For the plop of horses' feet on unpaved roads,
For the cry of bridges voicing their complaints
Through chattering planks beneath the horse-drawn loads.
I miss the creak of leather and the smell
Of weathered barns, the musty scent of hay,
The crunching sound of corn from darkened stalls,
A horse's sudden shrill and startled neigh.
Our cars are arrows, silver-tipped for speed,
We reach the far-off places, yet have lost
The wealth of leisure that we once had known:
Life's calm tranquility—and at what cost!

Through olden dark-ceiled rooms the dancers met
In purple velvet and in silken lace,
And tripped the measure through with courtly grace,
To the metered music of the minuet.
And there were poets who could not forget
The lyric-haunted theme—who sought to trace
With ink and pen each dancer's fitted place.
And thus the sonnet's rhythmic lines were set.

An aristocrat, indeed, the sonnet goes:
A stately step, a bow, a finger kiss—
It moves a graceful minuet of rhyme,
And smoothly sweet the music of it flows,
A soothing thing and gentle—after this,
The syncopated unrest of our time.

He knows the ways of beasts and birds,
Who can distinguish them by song and cry,
Who knows the bright quicksilver life in streams,
The courses that the stars take through the sky,
May never have laid hand to books, yet he
Is sharing wisdom with Infinity.

He who works with sensitive deft hands
At any woodcraft will absorb the rain,
The sunlight, and the starlight, and the dew,
That entered in the making of its grain;
He should grow tall and straight and clean and good
Who daily breathes the essences of wood.

He who finds companionship in rocks,
And comfort in the touch of vine and leaf,
Who climbs a hill for joy, and shouts a song,
Who loves the feel of wind, will know no grief,
No loneliness that ever grows too great—
For he will never be quite desolate.

He shares, who is companioned long with these,
All ancient wisdoms and philosophies.

INDIAN FARMER

I watched an Indian at his primitive sowing:
He scattered the seed with a slowly out-thrust hand;
Across his harrowed acres he was going,
His shoulders shawled, his head bound with a band.
This first American had no need to hurry,
The land remained, and ever would be the same.
He had his faithful gods, why should he worry?
He had his squaw, and her oven's scarlet flame.

Should there be drought he would have no need to fear it,
He would climb the nearby hill and pray for rain;
Upon his adobe roof at night he would hear it,
And the rain god would walk through the rustling grain.
His corn would be tall for his growing sons to gather
When the autumn came with its smoke on hill and wood.
This stalwart native, no matter what the weather,
Will love his plot of ground, and find it good.

I shall walk today upon a high green hill,
I shall forget the walls and the roofs of the town;
This burden, strapped to my back, shall be unloosed,
And I shall leave it there when I come down.

Warm is the hill upon which I shall walk today,
Gold is the sun upon the close-cropped grass,
And something of the peace of grazing sheep
Shall permeate my being as I pass.

Something of the look within their eyes
Of upland pastures, and of clean wind blown:
The tranquil, trusting look of those who know
A shepherd watches, I shall make my own.

And I shall gather the little windflowers there,
And press their sweetness upon my heart to stay,
Then I shall go back to the walls and the roofs of the town,
Stronger than I have been for many a day.

I KNOW A LAND

I know a land of blowing silver grasses.
The memory runs like music in my mind,
Over and over again with bright insistence,
Long after its wide reach is left behind:
A green and silver music which keeps lifting
Its cadences forever toward the sun,
A wordless song of light and windy laughter,
Flung from the throats of grasses as they run.

Here in the city's snarl of brick and mortar,
Its darkened canyons with their fevered dreams,
I still can hear that clear bright silver singing,
I still can see a wide land as it gleams;
And swift as a homing bird, released through light,
My spirit, seeking its own, takes sudden flight.

Dewy-eyed and shining-faced the morning
Is starting on its journey of today,
Its old wounds healed and seemingly forgotten,
Its old scars wiped away.

This brave new world! How staunchly it arises
From out the darkened covers of the night;
How valiantly it girds itself to enter
The splendid ways of light!

So would I shake the darkness from my eyelids,
So would I don my garments with the dawn,
The old wounds healed, the old scars unremembered,
And thus I would move on

Into the waiting ways of light and splendor,
My heart's bright banner lifted and unfurled,
That I may be a valiant marching comrade
To this, the brave new world.

THE LIGHT ON THE FARTHEST HILLS

Though the valley be dark with shadows,
And hushed be the singing rills,
O Heart, behold in the distance,
The light on the farthest hills.

The light! the light you are seeking!
Lift up your tired eyes
And glimpse it beyond the hilltops:
The blue of the clearing skies.

Let us forget the valley
And the long road that we came,
Let us move out and upward
Toward that golden flame.

Oh, let us leave behind us
The doubt, the fear and the dread:
There is God's glorious promise;
The light on the hills ahead!

Sometimes a longing for an adequate word
Clutches my heart
As if a hand were pressed
Tight on my breast.

It is said that the Japanese
Have one word for the blue of the sky after rain;
A word for the fluted look of wind-swept grain
Down any field.

Had I word for this pale tea-rose light
Along the east before the winter night
Drops its silvered blackness on the land,
I think perhaps the hand
Clutching my heart would loose its desperate hold.

Must I grow old
Never able to say at all
What a winter evening says to me?
Its twilight, clear as a crystal ball,
And still
As that great star over the hill;
The blue-white shadows, and the rosy light,
That comes for a brief moment before night,
Then goes, soft-feathered and swift as a winging bird?
Oh, for a word!

When all the poets of the earth have flung
Their ecstasies upon the listening air,
Poems too sweet for any heart to bear
Will cling above old fields and wait—unsung.
Beyond the spaces where the stars are swung
The jealous years will hold forever there
The old amaze, the rapture and despair
To which no poet yet has given tongue.

I need no longer hurry then to make
My small cool songs, for none can take from me
The steadfast sweetness of the blue hill mist,
The ancient wonder that the white stars wake.
There will be poems through eternity,
With God—the ultimate anthologist.

I SHALL BE YOUNG AGAIN

I shall be young again some heavenly day,
And I, who have loved beauty so, will be
As beautiful in a white shining way
As the flash of a gull's wings over a stormy sea!

I shall be light as a feather—I shall run
Across the cool green pastures of the sky:
A playmate of the heady winds, the sun,
And no one will be gladder there than I.

And none shall know the twisted roads I came,
Nor dream how slowly I have gone, for then
Swift as a swallow, quick as a lifting flame
I shall be beautiful—I shall be young again.

TULIP BULBS

Handle them carefully, gardener! these brown husks
Have banked their fires, but any moment may
Burst into flame. They hold the dawns and dusks
And the gold noons of every gorgeous day—
They are heavy with age, yet youth will rend them apart,
And color will tear its bright way through their heart.

A breathless interim they now are stilled,
But, gardener, you are dealing with mystery;
These globes encircle magic and are filled
With the wonder of things that were and that are to be.
Slip them quickly under the broken sod,
Lest you, too soon, come face to face with God.

A century of growth, of sun and rain,
Of calm and tempest, lie within the grain
That marks the lovely arms of this old chair.
I move a finger tip and trace them there
Within the curls of light: the running lines,
The darkened surface of the wood that shines,
And marvel greatly that I should possess
In my small house such hoarded loveliness;
That I should have and hold for beauty's sake
A thing God took a century to make.

SCENTS

I bruise a sprig of fir—a spray of pine,
Or crush a bit of balsam in my hands,
And in that lurking fragrance I can find
The forests of all lands.

If I were deaf and blind, and one should start
A sudden plow down furrows to be sown,
The odor rising there would bring again
All lost fields I have known.

A wet wind blows across the land at dusk,
Within its tang the seas of all the earth,
And I, born inland, hold my breath to catch
What I have sought since birth.

Oh, sight and sound, oh, beauty seen and heard,
You have not the incredible, strange power
To bring me joy or pain as does the scent
Of one small, book-pressed flower.

It takes so little to put back the heart
In any one: a loving word of praise,
Uttered sincerely, oftentimes may start
A light like sunshine running through the days.

It takes so little when the heart is sad
To lift it up—some bright encouragement
May reach the sorrowing one and make him glad,
Even when seemingly all hope is spent.

It takes so little, why should we withhold
That precious thing within our power to give?
Love, like a warm garment in the cold,
And sympathy for others while we live?

It takes so little, ah, dear God, I pray,
Help us to give it wisely day by day.

THE LONELY GRANDEURS

In following the swift onrush of the throng
We lay waste our powers and we spend
Strength we sorely need to keep us strong
To the far journey's end.

We forget the quietude we need:
The lonely grandeur of a place apart
Where manna will be sent on which to feed
To stay the hungry heart.

There we can cultivate the golden grain
Of honesty, integrity, and truth
From the idle, wasteland ground that may have lain
Fallow from our youth.

There are the lonely grandeurs to be found
By all who seek a quiet place to pray.
From our own mountainside God's voice will sound
Clearly out today.

These things are ageless, timeless, they belong
To the eternal verities and hold
The power of healing and the lift of song,
Yet they are young as the morning—and as old.
Cities have sunken into dust, great trees
Decay and fall beneath the wind and rain,
And nations have dissolved to naught, but these
Remain unchanged, and ever shall remain:
The mountains, standing stark against the sky,
The stars that nightly go their quiet way,
The constant resurrection of the shy
Sweet flowers that dot the land, unchanged, today,
And always the human heart with its desires,
Its hopes and fears, its conflicts and its fires.

Let us not forget the ancient wisdom
With which our fathers walked their earthly days:
The saying of grace above a loaf, new-broken;
The Sabbath rest; the altars we should raise:
The teaching of our faith to these, our children;
The earnest study of God's holy Word;
The constant telling of the old sweet story
By which an apathetic world is stirred.

Let us not forget the ancient splendors:
The mountaintop experience that lights
The darkest valleys that our feet must travel,
Where God will be, as well as on the heights.
Let us not forget the old, old meaning
Of the sun and moon and stars above the land.
Considering these, we ever would remember
That we, like they, are held in God's great hand.

Here is a woman's labor come to birth;
Here she is repaid for time and toil:
A blinding brilliance overflows the earth
And runs like light above the broken soil.
The heady phlox, the flaming marigolds,
The pungent gay nasturtiums in their bed
Toss in the wind—one single poppy holds
Color enough to dye the landscape red.
A woman's hands, a garden—a few seed,
And a wealth at last to meet the spirit's need.

How good are all the useful things of earth!
A plow, a mixing bowl, a tended hearth,
An auger and a hammer, saw and plane,
The clear glass of a polished windowpane,
Unvarnished lumber piled for future need—
Oh, all of these are beautiful, indeed:
The implements of labor that men's hands
Have used for centuries throughout all lands;
The ancient tried materials, the wood
And metals that have long been proven good—
These elemental things that came to be
The essence of the earth's great poetry.

Red-cheeked, deep-bosomed, wide of hips,
With laughter on her lips,
And strength in her good arms, her work but play,
And her small house on any day
Sanded and scrubbed, and sweet with the fresh smell
Of soap and coarse bleached linen. A pink shell
Filled with the sea's sounds props an open door,
A square of sunlight gilds the barren floor;
Through starched and ruffled curtains, snowy white,
The pewter pieces on her shelf take light,
While on her sill one vivid scarlet bloom
Sheds its pungent fragrance through the room.

And in a cradle, her small healthy son,
The image of the one
Who comes at night (as men of all lands do),
His day's work through,
To whom she lifts wide gladdened eyes abrim
With all her woman's love for him.

So long as there are homes to which men turn
At the close of day,
So long as there are homes where children are—
Where women stay,
If love and loyalty and faith be found
Across these sills,
A stricken nation can recover from
Its gravest ills.

So long as there are homes where fires burn
And there is bread,
So long as there are homes where lamps are lit
And prayers are said;
Although a people falters through the dark
And nations grope,
With God himself back of these little homes
We still can hope.

THE FIRST WILD ASTERS

The first wild asters, lovely though they be,
Have always sent a stabbing pain through me.
Their deep dark purple fills me with surprise;
Surely, I think, some fancy blinds my eyes;
Surely not yet, not yet should they appear
When it is so early in the year!

Always I have thought the summer done
When the wild asters' blossoming has begun.
Here I have found one in the wayside grass;
How swift, how very swift the seasons pass!
Time marked by tulips, violets, the rose—
Wild asters now—how swift, how swift life goes!

GENERATIONS

What shall we leave behind us, carved in stone,
Or graven on the hearts and minds of men:
This generation that must stand alone;
A brief life span that will be speaking when
The night comes down, and the paths that we have trod
Stretch out behind us in the sunset light?
What shall we leave behind us? Oh, dear God,
May it be clear-cut, fine—may it be right!

Something to make life simpler for those
Who follow after us, that they may find
A pointing finger, or a sign that shows
Where danger lies. God help us keep in mind
These young and valiant ones, with proud heads raised,
Who are to follow paths that we have blazed.

This is a holy time—be still, be still;
A child's white prayer is winging its sure way
Up to the throne of God. Across the sill
The last red light fades from the winter day,
As a young mother who is very wise
Is teaching a child to pray.

Two tall white candles burn beside her chair,
Piercing the dusk; they center in the eyes
Of the kneeling child like twin stars shining there;
They glimmer through the twilight of the room,
And make a halo of the mother's hair.

Brighter than the candles or the sunset light
Will be the fruit born of this precious hour.
The planted seed of faith will bear a white
Incredible flower,
And trust implanted in a child's heart may
Bear wonder-fruit some future day.
Oh, teach her well to pray!

Far on the Alpine slopes as the sun is setting
Its evening fires, and the peaks are gold with flame,
It is said that the shepherds have a quaint custom of singing
A song of the Lord's help, and praise to His name.
They call to each other across the twilit valleys,
Their flocks before them taking their homeward way,
Their voices lifting in beautiful benediction
To cheer and comfort their hearts at the close of day:

"Hitherto the Lord hath helped us. Let us praise Him,"
Echo on echo, clear as a harp's struck string,
Leaps from the peaks until all the air is vocal
With music, then faint and far their voices ring:
"Goodnight, goodnight," and the crags again make answer:
"Goodnight," and the dusk comes down . . .
Oh, I wish the same
Sweet song could echo across today's deep twilights:
"Hitherto the Lord hath helped, let us praise His name."

Out of the ivory palaces He came:
Jesus, our Lord, into the world, so poor
That His only fire was a star's cold flame,
His only welcome was an inn's closed door.
He came, the royal Heir of Heaven's Own,
To become the Son of man that we might be
The sons of God. He trod the earth alone
That we might proudly walk with royalty.

All hail the white incomparable Christ!
All hail the holy One, the sinless Lord!
The swiftly moving years have not sufficed
To give mankind the precious jeweled word
That will express the honor that we owe
To the humble Christ born centuries ago.

THE INNKEEPER'S LAMENT

They told me afterward there was a light
That shone night long above my khan's low roof,
Centering above the stable, radiant, white;
They tell me now it was a heavenly proof
That the Christ whom we had waited for so long
Was there . . . that I had turned Him from my door.
They say above the fields there was a song
Such as mankind had never heard before.

How could I know—how could I hear or see
Other than the clamor of the crowd,
The bleating sheep, the bartering cries, the queer
And sharp demands upon me that were loud?
If they had only told me! If they had,
I would have turned the other guests away.
I believe that every one would have been glad
For the stable's shelter and a bed of hay
To give the Christ Child room . . . Oh, surely I
Shall not be known forever as the one
Who shut his ears to a woman's needy cry,
Who closed his door upon God's holy Son.

SPARROWS

I love the sparrows, bad though they may be,
And you would love them, too, if you had lain
Long hours with them alone for company,
And if their friendliness had eased your pain.
Gray days, gray skies, gray sparrows on bare trees,
Yet something in their tuneless song so true,
I often think a sparrow's voice must please
The Lord as much as larks' and thrushes' do.

Remember this—"Are not two sparrows sold
For one small farthing, yet not one may fall
Without the Father sees it." This I hold
More close than any comforting at all.
"And fear ye not, therefore—" O little birds,
Your nearness brings the solace of these words.

The morning came, a piper,
And whistled me from bed.
I rose to brew my pot of tea
And break my loaf of bread,
But the gay, the bright insistence
Of that whistle sounding clear
And high outside my open door
Was all that I could hear.

I set my kettle back before
It had begun to sing
I left my loaf unbroken quite,
And walked a path in spring:
A little feathered, dewy path,
And high—a hidden bird
Reiterated often one
Clear shining silver word,
"Sweetheart, Sweetheart . . ." my loaf forgot,
My tea untouched by flame,
I walked the wood as one who hears
A long unuttered name.

I have never known but joy in coming home:
Rounding the corner down the last long lane,
Spying the chimney red against the foam
Of moving boughs, the golden windowpane
Catching the late light, and at last my feet
Ringing and quick upon the walk once more;
The scent of flowers somewhere, fragrant, sweet,
And my eager hand upon the opening door!

Now with the late light falling on the road,
Why should the homing heart be aught but glad?
Surely my shoulders need to ease their load;
Surely the journey's end should not be sad.
God grant some evening, the last signpost past,
My heart will lift its glad cry: "Home at last!"

Now that the Christ is risen,
Now with the darkness gone,
The road lies out before us,
Upward, and on and on.

There are His sandal footprints,
There is His form ahead,
Straight and strong and compelling,
The Christ that they left as dead.

Nothing can dim His glory,
Nothing can stay His feet,
And countless are they who follow
Him down each lane and street;

And I would be one among them,
Along the Glory Way;
I would arise and follow
The risen Christ today.

I heard God's voice upon the wind today;
I heard Him speaking through the song of birds;
And clearly, plainly, through the silver rain
I heard His words.

I saw God's face upon a flower today;
I saw Him moving on the hills, and oh,
He walked upon the water of the stream,
I know! I know!

I heard God's voice, I saw His shining face;
He spoke to me; He moved along the land;
I reached through all the beauty of the day
And touched His hand.

"The Lord thy God in the midst of thee is mighty,"
The words shine out—and suddenly I feel
That I, who have been weak and far too fearful,
Am armored with bright steel.

"The Lord thy God in the midst of thee is mighty,"
I shall not fail whatever may betide.
His might, His strength, His power is in my being,
And He moves by my side.

"The Lord thy God in the midst of thee is mighty,"
O men, lay steadfast hold upon that truth.
It will be staying comfort for the aged,
And a forceful strength for youth.

O righteous nations, claim that proffered power.
It will not fail you in your crucial hour.

207

The pure white fire of beauty burns forever.
Cities may be blasted from the earth
And the cherished homes of men be felled; but never
Can loveliness be lost. The gentle mirth
Of wind goes rippling through the tawny grasses,
New flowers blossom from the latter rains;
All that is tortuous and ugly passes,
But beauty—beauty remains.

Life's troubled waters cannot quench that fire.
Men's hate can never blur the sun's gold light,
Nor mar the moon's pale silver, as still higher
The steadfast stars climb up earth's darkest night;
And love, long crushed within the hearts of men,
Will rise—will rise again!

ORDER

I like to think that sometime life will be
Safe and sane once more; that we may find
Peace again, and the old tranquility
Of heart and mind:

I like to think of order on the earth;
Of order in the homes where women move,
Folding clean linens, keeping a glowing hearth
For those they love:

I like to think that horrors will not last;
That men will till their fields and reap their grain
Unhurriedly, the driving fury past,
Never to come again:

I like to think the air, itself, will clear
And bear us only music, sweet and low—
The evil tidings over, and the fear—
God grant it may be so.

WAIT

If but one message I may leave behind,
One single word of courage for my kind,
It would be this—Oh, brother, sister, friend,
Whatever life may bring, what God may send,
No matter whether clouds lift soon or late,
Take heart and wait.

Despair may tangle darkly at your feet,
Your faith be dimmed, and hope, once cool and sweet,
Be lost; but suddenly above a hill,
A heavenly lamp, set on a heavenly sill
Will shine for you and point the way to go,
How well I know.

For I have waited through the dark, and I
Have seen a star rise in the blackest sky
Repeatedly—it has not failed me yet.
And I have learned God never will forget
To light His lamp. If we but wait for it,
It will be lit.

210

Red bird, red bird, whistling on a tree,
You are all the flame and fire that have burned in me;
You are all the passion and the rapture I have known,
You are all my heartbreak whistling there alone.

Red bird, red bird, there is much to do,
I have not a moment's time to be watching you!
Now you go, but oh, that flame against the sky,
It is not a red bird, it is I.

SILENCE

Strange how still these things
Forever are:
The sun, the earth as it swings,
A journeying star;
And the sod with its leafy joys
Makes no noise.

Strange that the heart can break
Without a sound,
And in its desolate wake
No wound be found.
And the deepest grief in the breast
Is the quietest.

The greatest love through the years
May be left untold.
How silent are the tears
Of the very old!
But death is the stillest thing
That time will bring.

How shall my voice speak after I am gone
Into the company of the ever living?
I shall not leave behind a silent void
Remembering me no more, I shall be giving
Utterance still to some persistent speech.
And shall they, listening, say: "Our friend is voicing
Her bravest song of courage and of cheer.
The same sweet song she sang while she was here"?

How shall my voice speak after I am gone?
Shall they not say: "Our friend loved life and laughter,
And all the little gentle things of earth:
Bright April rains and sunshine coming after,
And flowers on the hills and homes at night?"
And shall they say: "We know our friend remembers,
For often, when the wind is down the slope,
We hear her voice, like some far beckoning hope?"

God grant my voice speaks thus when I am gone.
Harking backward from the starry places,
Grant it may cheer some traveler faring on,
That they who listen turn with lifted faces,
And eye grown luminous—because I speak.
God help me that I ever may remember
When each new day I sing my song again,
That as I now sing, so shall I sing then.

Hail and farewell . . . too brief the salutation;
Too soon the final handclasp and adieu.
A moment by a stile, or at a crossroad,
We meet and greet, then I go on, and you
Are lost somewhere among the mist and shadows,
Taking your own inevitable way
Along some distant road I cannot follow;
Into some distant day.

Hail and farewell . . . too soon the words are spoken,
Their sound, like some far-echoing silver bell . . .
O friend, O lover, comrade, sister, brother,
Hail and farewell!